WORDPRESS

665 Free WordPress Plugins for Creating Amazing and Profitable Websites

Create. Publish. Profit.

By Chad Tennant

WordPress Essentials. Copyright © 2015, 2016, and 2017.

All rights reserved.

The information in this book is for general reference and educational purposes only. This publication is not intended to provide tailored recommendations nor is it a basis for actions without careful analysis and due diligence. The ideas in this book may not be suitable for every individual. Neither the author nor the published are liable for any actions promoted or caused by the information presented in this book. Any views expressed herein are those of the author and do not represent the opinions of others.

Remember to back up your website/database regularly, and before installing any plugins as a best practice and safety precaution.

See Which 20+ Plugins I Use for My Sites

http://www.chadtennant.com/my-plugins

Amazon-Kindle Matchbook Program

If you buy a new print edition of this book (or purchased one in the past), you can get the Kindle Edition for FREE. Print edition purchase must be sold by Amazon.
The E-book version features clickable links.

Contents

INTRODUCTION 7

WORDPRESS.ORG VS. WORDPRESS.COM 9

THE WORDPRESS COMMUNITY 11

WORDPRESS TRAINING 13

SEARCH ENGINE OPTIMIZATION (SEO) 14

FREE AND PAID PLUGINS AND THEMES 17

HOW MANY PLUGINS ARE TOO MANY? 20

TOP FIVE PREMIUM PLUGINS 21

THE 665 BEST FREE PLUGINS 25

    AD INSERT & MANAGEMENT PLUGINS (8) 25

    ANALYTICS & STATISTICS PLUGINS (15) 27

    BACKUP PLUGINS (10) 29

    CACHE PLUGINS (WEBSITE SPEED) (7) 31

    CALENDAR & EVENT PLUGINS (10) 33

    CAPTCHA PLUGINS (5) 35

    CONTACT PLUGINS (17) 36

    CONTENT MANAGEMENT PLUGINS (24) 39

    COMMENT & SPAM MANAGEMENT PLUGINS (9) 42

    COMMUNICATION PLUGINS (3) 43

    COMMUNITY & MEMBERSHIP PLUGINS (8) 44

    E-COMMERCE & WOOCOMMERCE PLUGINS (22) 45

    E-MAIL & SMTP PLUGINS (20) 48

    FORM BUILDER & POPUPS PLUGINS (15) 51

    FAVICON (3) 53

    FONT PLUGINS (7) 53

    GOOGLE RELATED PLUGINS (5) 54

    IMAGE & MEDIA PLUGINS (53) 55

    LANGUAGE & TRANSLATION PLUGINS (9) 62

    LOGIN PLUGINS (11) 63

    MAP PLUGINS (13) 65

    MISCELLANEOUS (27) 67

POLLS, RATING, AND SURVEY PLUGINS (8) 70

POPULAR, RECENT, & RELATED POST PLUGINS (11) 72

REDIRECTION & LINK MANAGEMENT PLUGINS (24) 74

SECURITY PLUGINS (35) 77

SEO & SEARCH PLUGINS (15) 82

SHORTCODE & CODE PLUGINS (9) 84

SITE ADMINISTRATION PLUGINS (81) 85

SITE UNAVAILABLE & UNDER CONSTRUCTION PLUGINS (10) 95

SITEMAP PLUGINS (11) 97

SLIDER PLUGINS (9) 99

SOCIAL MEDIA & SHARING PLUGINS (42) 101

TABLE & DATABASE PLUGINS (2) 107

TERMS, SITE INFO, AND COOKIE PLUGINS (8) 108

USER MANAGEMENT PLUGINS (10) 109

VISUAL EDITOR, PAGE BUILDER, CSS, & THEME PLUGINS (41) 111

WEBSITE PERFORMANCE & SPEED PLUGINS (10) 116

WIDGET & SIDEBAR PLUGINS (33) 117

YOUTUBE & VIDEO PLUGINS (5) 121

BEST FREE IMAGE WEBSITES **122**

JOB SITES FOR WEB DEVELOPERS AND DESIGNERS **123**

INTRODUCTION

With over 50,000 plugins, WordPress offers its users many amazing choices to optimize, secure, and enhance their websites. Explore the 665 best plugins available to you!

In 2009, I sought web design services. It was the first time I required a website for a financial blog I was starting. I didn't have a clue how to set up a website, so I hired someone in my network to assist. After the creation of three sample sites and mounting expenses, I decided that learning how to create websites would be very useful. I was right. The designer used WordPress, so I started to learn more about it.

Seven years later, I've created many websites—some good and some bad—and I've enjoyed evolving with WordPress. WordPress is easy to use, yet amazingly powerful and practical. Best of all, I still don't know or need to know how to code with WordPress. If I've learned anything, the ability to create websites quickly is an extremely important tech-business skill to possess. Knowing how to design and develop a functional website provides endless self-employment and remote working opportunities.

WordPress is a free open-source software and content management system (CMS). Users can access thousands of themes and plugins to develop their websites. A theme is a website template and framework that can be customized by its user. A plugin extends the functionality of a website in any number of categories such as security, image management, search engine optimization, social media and so on.

WordPress powers <u>27.8%</u> of all websites and leads the way in content management systems with a market share of 58.9%. You can visit <u>Wikipedia</u> for more details.

With 50,000 plus plugins and growing, everyone has their favorites. Deciding on which plugins to use is very much a trial, error, and fun experiment. I have tracked down the best free plugins in over thirty different categories since no such listed existed. I searched high and low and page after page to bring you the best of the best.

There are many articles featuring the "best," "must have," and "top" plugins all over the web, but none of them are as comprehensive as my list. This book is your ultimate reference guide. This list of 665 plugins represents roughly 1.3% of all WordPress plugins currently available.

Have fun exploring these plugins and learning more about WordPress with new sections and categories that have been added.

To your success!

Chad Tennant, WordPress Enthusiast

WORDPRESS.ORG VS. WORDPRESS.COM

There can be some confusion between WordPress.org and WordPress.com, so let's understand their differences.

WordPress.org provides free open-source software to run a website, blog, or app. Also, it acts as an information repository for all things WordPress. There, you can find plenty of information and resources regarding themes, plugins, documentation, and support.

In tandem with the software, you'll need a hosting provider—the company that will keep your website up and running on the internet. WordPress.org recommends DreamHost (the provider I use), Bluehost, and SiteGround. However, you may choose a different provider as thousands exist. For example, GoDaddy.

With DreamHost, as well as others, the installation of WordPress software is achieved through a one-click installation process. Hosting usually cost around ten dollars a month depending on the provider. Furthermore, you can purchase and renew a domain name for about ten to fifteen dollars annually. For instance, www.yourdomain.com.

The open-source environment of WordPress.org attracts thousands of developers who create free themes and plugins for everyone to use. This produces amazing design and development options without any restrictions. However, user support can be hit or miss depending on the developer.

WordPress.com offers WordPress software, hosting, support, and limited themes and plugins all in one place. It's a one-stop-shop managed by Automattic—a website development company. The founder of Automattic, Matt Mullenweg, is also the founder of the WordPress software and foundation that runs WordPress.org.

WordPress.com **controls** which themes and plugins users have access to so your choices are far more limited. For example, you can't add plugins from this book since you won't find a "plugins tab" on your WordPress.com dashboard. Furthermore, WordPress.com offers only about 380 themes which pales in comparison to the thousands available via WordPress.org. That said, WordPress.com's assortment of themes and plugins satisfy most customers.

You can get a free website a WordPress.com if you don't mind using an address such as *yourname.**wordpress**.com* (search engines such as Google likely won't index/rank this). For a unique domain name, you'll have to pay as you would with any hosting provider.

Automattic manages technical issues, and they offer direct customer support. WordPress.com is ideal for people who want convenience and who don't mind operating in a closed environment with fewer theme and plugin options. I liken WordPress.org to Google's Android operating software, and WordPress.com to Apple's iOS.

If you don't have a website, like having options, or are just entering the fantastic world of WordPress, I recommend going with WordPress.org. By doing so, you'll be able to access all the plugins in this book and much more.

THE WORDPRESS COMMUNITY

Thousands of WordPress users flock to WordPress.org for support. However, support and social interactions are available on other websites and face-to-face.

Facebook

There are many WordPress groups and several that I've joined. Some groups allow members to discuss all things WordPress compared with groups that focus on particular topics. For example, a group that discusses plugins only. Therefore, it's important to understand a group's rules and guidelines before posting to avoid getting banned.

To find WordPress groups, type "WordPress" in the Facebook search bar, select "Groups," and explore. I tend to gravitate toward groups that have a minimum of five thousand members and an engaged administrator who controls spam.

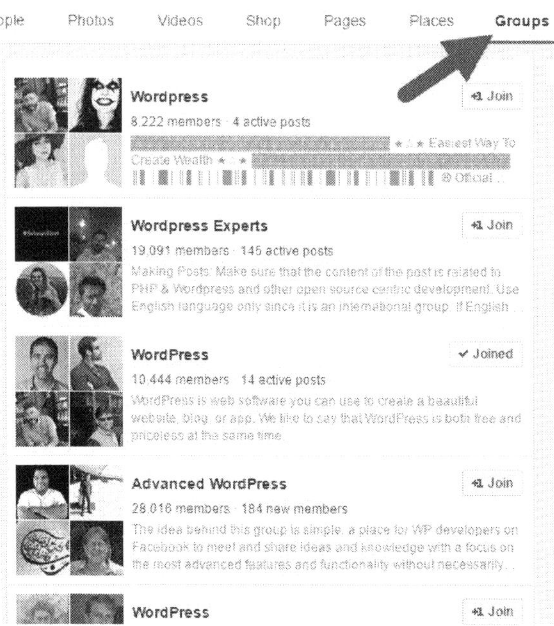

WordCamp

WordCamps are casual, locally-organized conferences covering everything related to WordPress. WordCamps come in all different flavors, based on the local communities that produce them, but in general, WordCamps include sessions on how to use WordPress more effectively, beginning plugin and theme development, advanced techniques, security, and so on. To get an idea of the types of sessions typically seen at WordCamps, check out the WordCamp channel at WordPress.tv.

WordCamps are attended by people ranging from blogging newbies to professional WordPress developers and consultants. WordCamps combine scheduled programming with conference sessions and other activities.

WORDPRESS TRAINING

WordPress is super easy to use since it doesn't necessitate extensive coding, web development, or computer skills. The WordPress framework makes developing and managing websites straightforward. However, there is tremendous value in learning about WordPress through online courses and tutorials. For example, a new user of WordPress software should consider taking a beginner's course to save him or herself from some wasteful trial and error. Also, as an experienced WordPress user, I occasionally watch tutorials on YouTube to learn about best practices.

There are plenty of free learning resources on the web with Codex—WordPress's information support library—leading the way. YouTube is another fantastic option to watch how-to videos. For example, how to design a WordPress website. Finally, popular e-learning platforms such as Skillshare, Treehouse, and others offer free and paid online courses regarding WordPress and web development.

WordPress Blogs

There are dozens of WordPress authority sites covering news, reviews, tips, tricks, and tutorials. I visit some from time to time as an alternative to YouTube. Elegant Themes (Divi/Bloom) has a list of twenty-two WordPress blogs worth exploring. Furthermore, you can visit these top ranked sites for WordPress tips, insights, and more.

- WPBeginner
- WPExplorer
- WPMudev
- ManageWP
- WPKube

SEARCH ENGINE OPTIMIZATION (SEO)

Search engine optimization (SEO), you know what it is or are familiar with the concept, but is learning it important to you? SEO has always been a fascination of mine but had never been a full-blown priority until last year.

I follow a simple mantra, **if nobody can see or find you, nobody will buy you**. In other words, if your posts, products, and services show up on the ninth page of Google search results, it will be difficult to attract traffic/visitors to your website (no/low traffic = no/low sales). Therefore, understanding and implementing SEO activities can lead to attracting more visitors and sales.

Many studies highlight the importance of being on the first page of search results. Call it convenience or laziness, most searchers limit their clicks to page one results. According to <u>Philip Petrescu</u>, "On average, 71.33% of searches result in a page one organic click. Page two and three get only 5.59% of the clicks. On the first page alone, the first five results account for 67.60% of all the clicks and the results from 6 to 10 account for only 3.73%."

Learning about SEO and applying the best practices won't guarantee top rankings. However, it will provide you with strategic advantages and allow you to pick SEO battles more wisely. For example, I've chosen not to write about certain topics because those posts would not likely rank well given the existing competition.

Who Should Learn SEO

Although SEO is just one of many online marketing activities, it's the most critical to learn. Understanding SEO obviously helps with ranking in search engines, but it also helps with ranking wherever search is applicable. For example, on Amazon. You should learn SEO if you:

- Own or manage a website or blog
- Conduct internet marketing activities–affiliate, content, social media, video, and so on
- Generate revenue through online marketplaces–Amazon, eBay, Fiverr, and Upwork
- Value SEO/SEM as part of your digital marketing strategy

SEO Training

Your goal should be to understand and implement viable and legitimate SEO strategies. Taking too many courses won't lead to a greater understanding of SEO because the law of diminishing return will quickly set in and data points will become redundant. I recommend referencing two or three courses and resources.

In a quest to learn SEO, a person can get easily overwhelmed by search results (the irony). Fortunately, my exposure to e-learning platforms enables to point you in the right direction.

Coursera provides global access to the world's best education, partnering with top universities and organizations to offer courses online. They've partnered with Stanford, Yale, and Princeton to name a few. Students can take courses for free or pay to obtain course completion certificates as I did for a marketing course I completed. Additionally, Coursera offers multi-course specializations in various subjects.

Coursera offers a robust six-course SEO specialization in partnership with the University of California. I'm currently enrolled, and after completing the first course, I was thoroughly impressed and look forward to taking the others. Moreover, I recommend paying for the program, if you wish to expand your career options or desire to become an SEO consultant.

Moz started in 2004 as an SEO consultancy and expanded in the same direction to offer a range of software as a service (SaaS) solutions. Their brand has become synonymous with SEO, and they're considered a global authority. In fact, a search for "what is SEO" yields two Moz results on page one—that's walking the walking.

Moz offers a treasure chest of online learning resources including guides, webinars (Mozinars), quizzes, whitepapers, and more at their website. I explored several of their resources which proved to be beneficial.

While Moz is synonymous with SEO, Google is synonymous with search. Google commands nearly two-thirds of US search activity, and they have an incredible global brand. Millions of online users prefer Google over their chief rivals, for example, Bing and Yahoo. Suffice it to say; most training resources structure their contents based on Google's search engine, algorithms, and announcements.

Google doesn't offer an SEO training course per se, but their brief SEO starter guide is a must read. I recommend reading it after you learn a few things about SEO. Furthermore, their suite of free tools including Google Analytics, Webmaster, AdWords, and others embody nuances to excel in SEO. For example, their free keyword planning tool found in AdWords is used by millions of SEO practitioners including myself. I rebooted my Webmaster account when I was reminded of its value through the Coursera course. Google offers free training for their various tools and platforms on websites such as YouTube.

There are several excellent WordPress SEO plugins including All-In-One-SEO and Yoast, but unless you understand SEO, these plugins **will prove useless**. Yoast offers the second most used SEO WordPress plugin, and for training purposes, they have an academy consisting of a blog, ebooks, and courses. Also, their YouTube channel is worth exploring.

SearchEngineJournal (SEJ) is my favorite topical website. They publish insightful articles such as "The Death of Organic Search (As We Know It)" and other content relating to online marketing. They offer a beginner's guide to SEO worth reading.

FREE AND PAID PLUGINS AND THEMES

With thousands of free plugins and themes on the market, why would anyone pay for either? Many free plugins and themes can meet your needs depending on your objectives and priorities. For example, a person setting up a blog will have different needs compared with someone setting up an e-commerce website.

Most of the time free plugins/themes will suffice, but on other occasions, they won't. For instance, if growing your email list is a critical objective, you'll want a robust opt-in form plugin to achieve desired results. While there are many free form and popup plugins, you may or may not be content with them. I wasn't content after trying several free form plugins, so I decided to invest in <u>Thrive Leads</u>.

Sometimes "free" can only take you so far or not far enough. Moreover, you may want features such as analytics, customer support, and enhanced customizeation which are usually associated with premium plugins and themes.

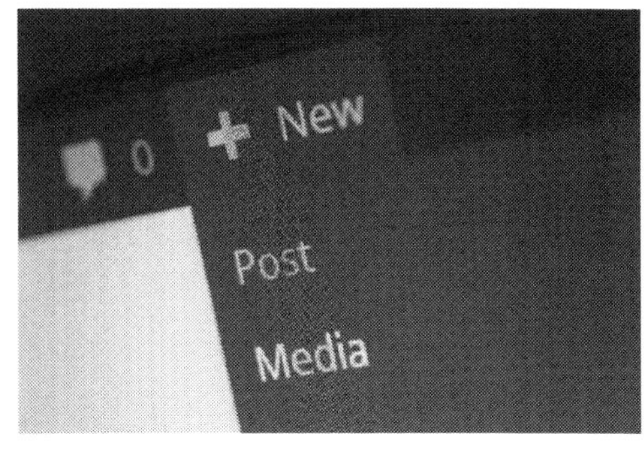

Many premium plugins and themes cost between twenty to one-hundred dollars, but these costs can add up quickly through trial and error and without a game plan.

When considering which free or paid plugins/themes to install, I recommend taking the following steps:

1. Before beginning your search for a plugin or theme, put on your project manager's hat and define your requirements. Consider and predetermine your objectives, needs, and

priorities for your website. Your thoughts and ideas don't need to be concrete, but it helps to start from a place of knowingness and objectivity.

2. Search for free plugins/themes within your WordPress dashboard and select four to six contenders. Install, activate, and evaluate them against your requirements. Narrow down your list to two selections and explore them further. If they don't meet your needs, repeat this step or consider searching for paid plugins/themes on the internet. If you take the latter step, purchase one theme at a time and experiment. If all else fails, review your requirements and make any necessary adjustments so that you can find a plugin/theme that meets your needs.

3. Review your requirements on an ongoing basis and if things change, repeat steps one and two.

General Public License (<u>GPLv2</u>)

"The licenses for most software are designed to take away your freedom to share and change it. By contrast, the GNU General Public License is intended to guarantee your freedom to share and change free software—to make sure the software is free for all its users. This General Public License applies to most of the Free Software Foundation's software and to any other program whose authors commit to using it." –WordPress.org

Only recently, did I engage in a debate about free versus paid plugins/themes in a Facebook group. It appears there are some hardcore WordPress users who believe paid solutions have no place in the open-source WordPress environment.

WordPress is an excellent platform, and users can find many exceptional free plugins/themes. However, WordPress is also a business opportunity that some web designers and developers want to capitalize on—I think they call this capitalism.

I'm glad I don't have to pay for every single plugin I use, but I'm happy to invest in my online business through premium plugins and themes that elevate my operations. GPL hippies must get over themselves and appreciate entrepreneurs seeking to deliver premium products that outperform free ones. People have bills to pay, and I appreciate entrepreneurs who seek to deliver game-changing products. If their solutions are worthwhile, they'll succeed. If their value propositions are weak, they'll fail.

How Many Plugins Are Too Many?

It's easy to go crazy with adding plugins to our sites, but how many is too many? I have around twenty-five installed on chadtennant.com, and every plugin serves a measurable purpose. According to Dan Norris of WP Curve, "As a general guide, we like to keep sites to under 20 plugins. A better rule of thumb is 'less is best.' If you can have zero, then that's fantastic but probably unrealistic. We have two recommendations here: remove any plugins you don't need and remove any inactive or active plugins that you don't need."

Between Dan and I, we may agree that having twenty to thirty plugins is enough to achieve desired backend and frontend goals. However, having fifty-three or 637 plugins are also possibilities.

Plugins can affect the backend and frontend of your site. This means they can provide a function that the site admin can take advantage of such as analytics, backups, and SEO or they can add a feature to the frontend for the benefit of visitors such as sliders, widgets, and forms.

Plugins impact site performance in two distinct ways: additional HTTP requests and additional database queries which ultimately impact factors such a website performance, page speed and loading times, security, and vulnerabilities associated with poorly coded or out-of-date plugins.

There are several ways to gauge your website-plugin status. For example, checking the speed of your site using Google's PageSpeed Insights. Also, the P3 (Plugin Performance Profiler) plugin measures the impact of plugins on site loading time. To get a general sense of how your site is scoring concerning various metrics, visit these sites.

- GTMetrix
- Pingdom
- SEO SiteCheckup
- Website Grader
- WPMUDEV

TOP FIVE PREMIUM PLUGINS

I love free plugins, and of the <u>twenty-something plugins</u> I use, all but one is paid—<u>Thrive Themes</u>. I strongly believe that one or two premium plugins can make a huge difference in an online business using WordPress.

Premium plugins attract fees for a reason, and usually, it's because they offer more than their free counterparts. For example, superior features or customer support. My recommendation is to experiment with free plugins until you believe purchasing a premium one will justify the cost. For instance, I tried SumoMe and MailMunch before implementing Thrive Leads for email capture and lead generation activities.

1. <u>Thrive Themes</u>

Thrive Themes offers a suite of marketing and lead capture plugins including opt-in forms, landing pages, countdown timers, and more. Users get various list building solutions at an affordable price. Thrive Themes offers:

- Thrive Leads: eleven types of opt-in forms including scroll mat, ribbon, screen filler, content lock, footer, and more.
- Thrive Landing Pages: over 160+ high converting sales, registration, and webinar pages.
- Content Builder: the fastest and most intuitive visual editor for WordPress. Easily create drag-and-drop layouts, add buttons, and advanced content elements.
- WordPress themes: ten high-converting and responsive themes.
- Additional plugins including Clever Widgets, Headline Optimizer, Thrive Ultimatum, Thrive Ovation, and Thrive Quiz Builder

2.   <u>Elegant Themes</u>

WordPress users love Divi, "the most popular premium WordPress theme in the world." Divi is extremely versatile and includes a visual drag and drop page builder. Also, Elegant Themes' <u>Bloom</u> plugin is an excellent alternative to Thrive Leads for lead capture and list building.

3.   <u>WP Rocket</u>

Caching is the best way to reduce the loading time of your site. You can Speed up your WordPress website easily and quickly with the WP Rocket caching plugin. Visit their <u>features page</u> to see how they compare against free plugins.

4.   <u>Cart66</u>

Cart66 adds e-commerce capabilities to your site with a huge list of features. Here are some of the most notable features:

- Offer shopping carts
- Sell digital files
- Shipping service integration
- Order updates for customers
- Inventory tracking
- Sales reports
- Coupons that can be auto-applied
- Automatic notification emails
- Sell on social media
- Affiliate programs
- Sell subscriptions
- Integrate with other services like MailChimp and Gravity Forms
- Wholesale store capability

There are many free e-commerce plugins, but Cart66 knocks them out of the park. It's all about the sheer number of fantastic features available under one roof. This plugin can help keep your site running fast since you won't have to install as many plugins as with other free plugins such as WooCommerce and WP eCommerce.

5.   <u>ManageWP</u>

If you are working with WordPress, chances are high that you are not only taking care of one site but several at the same time. Even with a platform as user-friendly as WordPress, this can be a hassle. For example, logging in, surfing each dashboard, performing updates, and other maintenance tasks.

ManageWP makes this process more streamlined by letting you take care of everything from one central location. From the dashboard, you can manage themes and plugins, create posts and pages, and update WordPress and its components on all your sites with just a few clicks. The plugin can even give you information about site uptime, access to Google analytics, and schedule site backups.

THE 665 BEST FREE PLUGINS

In the previous version of this book, I listed the top 500 free plugins. Now you have 665 at your disposal. Under the previous standard, a plugin made my list if it had a minimum of 100,000 downloads, several reviews, and a four-star rating or higher.

The WordPress.org directory now features "active installs" instead of how many times plugins are downloaded. So, inlusion in this list required a minimum of 30,000 active installs, close to ten reviews, and a four-star rating or higher.

In a moment, you're going to sift through many amazing plugins. As any seasoned WordPress user knows, some plugin categories are more critical than others. Website administration, backup, SEO, security, and page speed plugin categories should be top-of-mind regarding our sites.

Although not highlighted in traditional hyperlink blue, plugins listed are clickable and will take you to the plugin's homepage on WordPress.org. I left the grammar as is regarding titles and descriptions so you will find **plenty of grammatical errors**. I did this so that you can match what is listed here to the exact plugin.

Ad Insert & Management Plugins (8)

Quick AdSense   Clickable Hyperlink

Quick AdSense offers a quicker & flexible way to insert Google AdSense or any Ads.

AdRotate

The popular choice for monetizing your website with adverts while keeping things simple.

Ad Inserter

Insert any advert or code into WordPress. Perfect for all kinds of banners and ads…

AdSense Plugin WP QUADS

Quick Adsense Reloaded! Quickest way to insert Google AdSense & other ads into your website.…

Ad Injection

Injects any adverts (e.g. AdSense) into the WordPress posts or widget area. Restrict who sees…

Website Monetization by MageNet

Get additional income from your website or blog by placing text ads automatically.

Advanced Ads

Manage and optimize your ads and ads performance with support for AdSense, ad injection, ad…

Wp-Insert

The Ultimate Adsense / Ad-Management Plugin for WordPress

Analytics & Statistics Plugins (15)

Google Analytics for WordPress by MonsterInsights
The best Google Analytics plugin for WordPress.

Google Analytics Dashboard for WP
Displays Google Analytics stats in your WordPress Dashboard.

WP Statistics
Complete statistics for your WordPress site.

StatCounter – Free Real Time Visitor Stats
StatCounter.com powered real-time detailed stats about the visitors to your blog.

WP-PostViews
Enables you to display how many times a post/page had been viewed.

Slim Stat Analytics
Slim Stat Analytics

Count per Day

Visit Counter, shows reads and visitors per page, visitors today, yesterday, last week, last months.

WP-Piwik

This plugin adds a Piwik stats site to your WordPress or WordPress multisite dashboard.

Google Analytics Counter Tracker

Google analytics counter tracker – analyse the visitors hits on you website and display it.

NewStatPress

NewStatPress (Statpress plugin fork) is a real-time plugin to manage the visits' statistics about your.

Analytics

Analytics of Google: analytics code integration on WordPress website

Post Views Counter

Post Views Counter allows you to display how many times a post, page or custom…

GA Google Analytics

Adds your Google Analytics Tracking Code to your WordPress site.

Visitors Traffic Real Time Statistics

Best statistics plugin for WordPress to display your site statistics & traffic. Enable you to…

Statify

Visitor statistics for WordPress with focus on data protection, transparency and clarity. Perfect as a…

Backup Plugins (10)

UpdraftPlus WordPress Backup Plugin
UpdraftPlus simplifies backups (and restoration). Backup into the cloud (Amazon S3 (or compatible), Dropbox, Google Drive, Rackspace Cloud, DreamObjects, FTP, Openstack Swift, UpdraftPlus Vault and email) and restore with a single click.

Duplicator
Duplicate, clone, backup, move and transfer an entire site from one location to another.

BackWPup – WordPress Backup Plugin
The backup plugin BackWPup can be used to save your complete installation including /wp-content/ and push them to an external Backup Service, like Dropbox, S3, FTP and many more, see list below.

WP-DB-Backup
On-demand backup of your WordPress database.

BackUpWordPress
Simple automated backups of your WordPress-powered website.

Backup Guard – backup & restore
Backup, clone, migrate, duplicate and restore your website.

XCloner – Backup and Restore
Backup your site, restore to any web location, send your backups to Dropbox, Amazon S3.

WP Database Backup
Create & Restore Database Backup easily on single click. Manual or automated backups (backup to.

Backup & Restore Dropbox
Backup & Restore Dropbox Plugin to create Dropbox Full Backup (Files + Database) or Restore,…

Backup & Restore WPBackItUp
Backup, restore, clone, duplicate or migrate your site effortlessly with WPBackItUp.

Cache Plugins (Website Speed) (7)

WP Super Cache
A very fast caching engine for WordPress that produces static html files.

W3 Total Cache
W3 Total Cache improves the SEO and user experience of your site by increasing website performance, reducing download times via features like content delivery network (CDN) integration.

WP Fastest Cache
The simplest and fastest WP Cache system.

LiteSpeed Cache
varnish, litespeed web server, lsws, availability, pagespeed, woocommerce, bbpress, nextgengallery, wp-polls, wptouch, customization, plugin, rewrite.

Varnish HTTP Purge
Automatically purge Varnish Cache when content on your site is modified.

DB Cache Reloaded Fix
The fastest cache engine for WordPress, that produces cache of database queries with easy configuration....

Nginx Helper
Cleans nginx's fastcgi/proxy cache or redis-cache whenever a post is edited/published. Also does a few...

DB Cache Reloaded Fix
The fastest cache engine for WordPress, that produces cache of database queries with easy configuration....

Cleans nginx's fastcgi/proxy cache or redis-cache whenever a post is edited/published. Also does a few...

Calendar & Event Plugins (10)

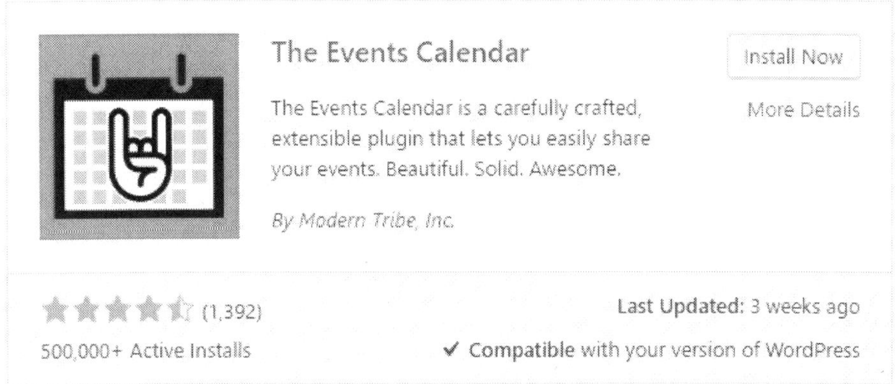

The Events Calendar
Create and manage your calendar of events with ease.

All-in-One Event Calendar
Calendar, ical, iCalendar, all-in-one, events sync, events widget, calendar widget.

Events Manager
Fully featured event registration management including recurring events, locations management, calendar, Google map integration, and more.

Comet Cache
Comet Cache is an advanced WordPress caching plugin inspired by simplicity.

Editorial Calendar
The Editorial Calendar makes it possible to see all your posts and drag and drop.

Event Organiser
Create and maintain events, including complex reoccurring patterns, venue management (with Google maps), calendars and…

Booking Calendar
Booking Calendar plugin – is the ultimate booking system for online reservation and availability checking…

Calendar by WD – Responsive Event Calendar for WordPress
Event Calendar plugin is a highly configurable product which allows you to have multiple organized…

My Calendar
Accessible WordPress event calendar plugin. Show events from multiple calendars on pages, in posts, or…

wp-jalali
Full Jalali calendar support for WordPress and localization improvements for Persian/Afghan/Tajik users.

CAPTCHA Plugins (5)

Really Simple CAPTCHA
Really Simple CAPTCHA does not work alone and is intended to work with other plugins.

Captcha by BestWebSoft
1 super security anti-spam captcha plugin for WordPress forms.
SI CAPTCHA Anti-Spam

Adds Secure Image CAPTCHA on the forms for comments, login, registration, lost password, BuddyPress, bbPress, and more.

Google Captcha (reCAPTCHA) by BestWebSoft
Protect WordPress website forms from spam entries with Google reCaptcha.

Better WordPress reCAPTCHA (with no CAPTCHA reCAPTCHA)
This plugin utilizes Google reCAPTCHA to help your blog stay clear of spams. BWP reCAPTCHA…

Contact Plugins (17)

Contact Form 7
Just another contact form plugin. Simple but flexible.

Ninja Forms
Ninja Forms is the ultimate free form creation tool for WordPress. Build forms within minutes using a simple yet powerful drag-and-drop form creator.

Fast Secure Contact Form
An easy and powerful form builder that lets your visitors send you email.

Contact Widgets
Beautifully display social media and contact information on your website with these simple widgets.

Contact Form by BestWebSoft
Simple contact form plugin any WordPress website must have.

Simple Contact Form Plugin – PirateForms
Makes your contact form page more engaging by creating a good-looking simple WordPress contact form.

Flamingo
A trustworthy message storage plugin for Contact Form 7.

Contact Form 7 Honeypot
Contact Form 7 Honeypot – Adds honeypot anti-spam functionality to CF7 forms.

Visual Form Builder
Build beautiful, fully functional contact forms in only a few minutes without writing PHP, CSS, and more.

Contact Form 7 Datepicker
Easily add a date field using jQuery UI's date picker to your CF7 forms. This plugin.

Contact Form by WPForms – Drag & Drop Form Builder for WordPress
The best WordPress contact form plugin.

Contact Form by WD – responsive drag & drop contact form builder tool
Contact Form by WD plugin is a simple contact form builder tool, which allows the

Contact Form 7 Dynamic Text Extension
This plugin provides 2 new tag types for the Contact Form 7 Plugin.

MW WP Form
MW WP Form is shortcode base contact form plugin. This plugin have many feature. For…

Contact Form Clean and Simple
A clean and simple AJAX contact form with Google reCAPTCHA, Twitter Bootstrap markup and Akismet…

Contact Bank – Contact Forms Builder
Contact Bank is an ultimate form builder WordPress plugin that lets you create contact forms…

Bootstrap for Contact Form 7
This plugin modifies the output of the popular Contact Form 7 plugin to be styled…

Content Management Plugins (24)

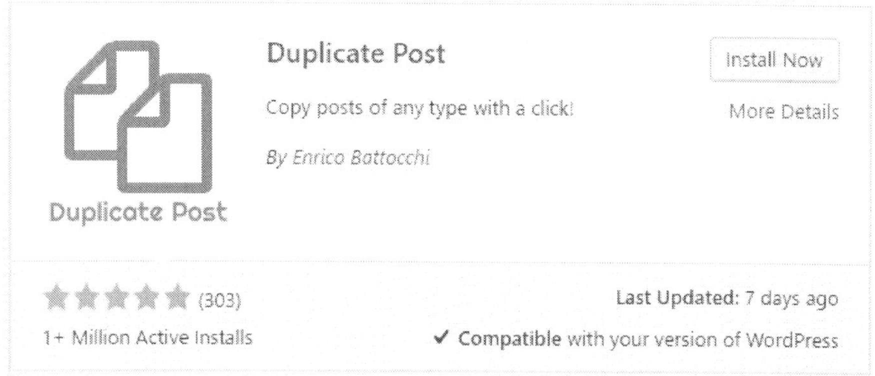

Duplicate Post
Clone posts and pages.

Breadcrumb NavXT
Adds breadcrumb navigation showing the visitor's path to their current location.

Duplicate Page
Duplicate Posts, Pages and Custom Posts easily using single click.

WP Edit
Take complete control over the WordPress content editor.

Slideshow
Integrate a fancy slideshow in just five steps.

Table of Contents Plus
A powerful yet user friendly plugin that automatically creates a table of contents.

Title Remover

Gives you the ability to hide the title of any post, page or custom post.

Insert PHP

Run PHP code inserted into WordPress posts and pages.

List Category Posts

List Category Posts allows you to list posts by category in a post or page using the [catlist] shortcode.

Hide Title

Allows authors to hide the title on single pages and posts via the edit post.

WP Easy Columns

Easy Columns provides the shortcodes to create a grid system or magazine style columns.

Advanced Excerpt

Control the appearance of WordPress post excerpts.

Collapse-O-Matic

Collapse-O-Matic adds an [expand title="trigger text"]hidden content[/expand] shortcode that will wrap any content, including other.

Post Expirator

Allows you to add an expiration date to posts which you can configure to either.

Post Type Switcher

A simple way to change a post's type in WordPress

Page-list
[pagelist], [subpages], [siblings] and [pagelist_ext] shortcodes

Custom Post Template
Provides a drop-down to select different templates for posts from the post edit screen.

Page scroll to id
Create links that scroll the page smoothly to any id within the document.

Pods – Custom Content Types and Fields
Pods is a framework for creating, managing, and deploying customized content types and fields.

Dynamic "To Top" Plugin
Adds an automatic and dynamic "To Top" button to easily scroll long pages back to…

Show Hide Author
Choose whether to show or hide the author's name.

Advanced iFrame
Include content the way YOU like in an iframe that can hide and modify elements…

Tabby Responsive Tabs
Create responsive tabs inside your posts, pages or custom post content by adding simple shortcodes…

WP Meta and Date Remover
Remove meta author and date information from posts and pages. Hide from Humans and Search…

Comment & Spam Management Plugins (9)

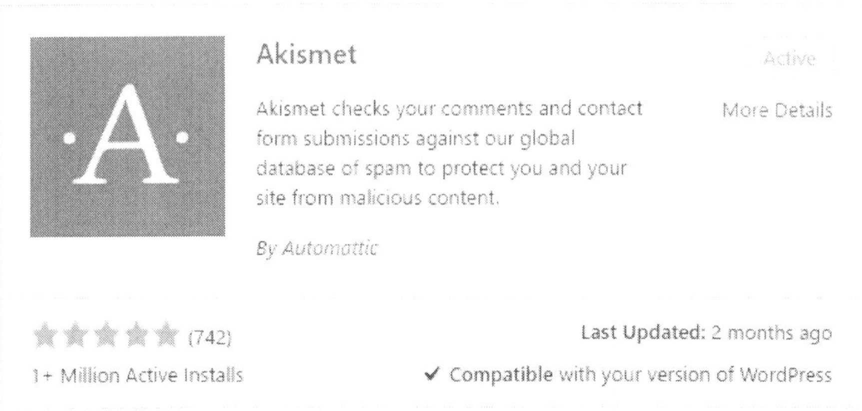

Akismet
Akismet checks your comments and contact form submissions against our global database of spam to prevent your site from publishing malicious content.

Disable Comments
Allows administrators to globally disable comments on their site.

Antispam Bee
Easy and extremely productive spam-fighting plugin with many sophisticated solutions.

Anti-spam
No spam in comments. No captcha.

Facebook Comments
Facebook comments can be annoying to set up. This plugin makes it simple to add the Facebook comments system to your WordPress site without any hassle.

Spam FireWall, Anti-Spam by CleanTalk
Spam protection, anti-spam, all-in-one, premium plug-in. No spam comments & users, no spam contact.

No Page Comment
An admin interface to control the default comment and trackback settings on new posts, pages…

Stop Spammers Spam Prevention
Aggressive anti-spam plugin that eliminates comment spam, trackback spam, contact form spam and registration spam.…

WP-SpamShield Anti-Spam – All-in-One Spam Protection
All-in-one WordPress spam protection, with NO CAPTCHAs, challenge questions or other inconvenience to site visitors.

Communication Plugins (3)

Zendesk Chat
Zendesk Chat (previously Zopim) lets you monitor and chat with visitors surfing your store.

Tawk.to Live Chat
(OFFICIAL tawk.to plugin) Instantly chat with visitors on your website with the free tawk.to chat.

Call Now Button
A very simple yet very effective plugin that adds a Call Now button to your.

Community & Membership Plugins (8)

bbPress
bbPress is forum software, made the WordPress way.

BuddyPress
BuddyPress helps site builders and WordPress developers add community features to their websites.

Members
The most powerful user, role, and capability management plugin for WordPress.

WP-Members: Membership Framework
WP-Members™ is a free membership management framework for WordPress® that restricts content to registered users.

Subscribe to Comments
Subscribe to Comments allows commenters on an entry to subscribe to e-mail notifications for subsequent.

Paid Memberships Pro
A revenue-generating machine for membership sites. Unlimited levels with recurring payment, protected content and member.

Ultimate Member
The easiest way to create powerful online communities and beautiful user profiles with WordPress

s2Member Framework (Member Roles, Capabilities, Membership, PayPal Members)
s2Member®—a powerful (free) membership plugin for WordPress®. Protect members only content with roles/capabilities.

E-Commerce & WooCommerce Plugins (22)

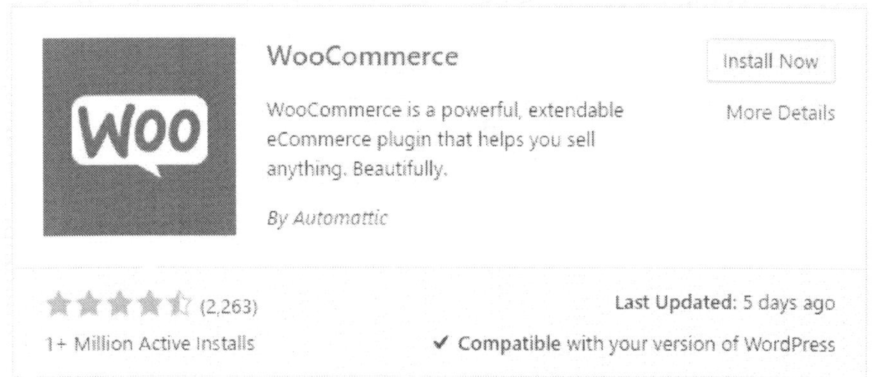

WooCommerce

WooCommerce is a powerful, extendable eCommerce plugin that helps you sell anything. Beautifully.

YITH WooCommerce Wishlist

YITH WooCommerce Wishlist add all Wishlist features to your website. Needs

WooCommerce to work.

WooCommerce Stripe Payment Gateway

Take credit card payments on your store using Stripe.

YITH WooCommerce Compare

YITH WooCommerce Compare allows you to compare more products of your shop in one complete.

YITH WooCommerce Zoom Magnifier

YITH WooCommerce Zoom Magnifier add zoom effect to product images and a customizable image slider.

YITH WooCommerce Ajax Product Filter
WooCommerce Ajax Product Filter lets you apply the filters you need to display the correct WooCommerce variations of the products you are looking for.

WordPress Download Manager
This File Management & Digital Store plugin which will help you to control file downloads

WooCommerce PDF Invoices & Packing Slips
Create, print & automatically email PDF invoices & packing slips for WooCommerce orders.

Easy Digital Downloads
The easiest way to sell digital products with WordPress.

WooCommerce Multilingual – run WooCommerce with WPML
Allows running fully multilingual e-commerce sites using WooCommerce and WPML.

YITH WooCommerce Quick View
This plugin adds the possibility to have a quick preview of the products right from…

WooCommerce Grid / List toggle
Adds a grid/list view toggle to product archives

WooCommerce Customizer
Helps you customize WooCommerce without writing any code!

WooCommerce Menu Cart
Automatically displays a shopping cart in your menu bar. Works with WooCommerce, WP-Ecommerce, EDD, Eshop…

WooCommerce Print Invoice & Delivery Note
Print invoices and delivery notes for WooCommerce orders.

Persian Woocommerce
This plugin extends the WooCommerce shop plugin with complete Persian(Farsi) language packs

WooCommerce PagSeguro
Adds PagSeguro gateway to the WooCommerce plugin

Saphali Woocommerce Russian
Набор русских дополнений к интернет-магазину на Woocommerce. Adds Russian localization & special Tools in WooCommerce.

Woocommerce CSV importer
Import products into woocommerce.

Booster for WooCommerce
Supercharge your WordPress WooCommerce site with these awesome powerful features.

WooCommerce Checkout Field Editor (Manager) Pro
WooCommerce Checkout Field Editor Pro – The best WooCommerce checkout manager plugin to customize checkout…

WooCommerce Products Filter
WooCommerce Products Filter – flexible, easy and robust professional filter for products in the WooCommerce…

E-Mail & SMTP Plugins (20)

WP Mail SMTP
The most popular SMTP plugin on WordPress.org. Trusted by over 600k sites.

MailChimp for WordPress
MailChimp for WordPress helps you add more subscribers to your MailChimp lists using various methods.

MailPoet Newsletters
Send newsletters post notifications or autoresponders from WordPress easily, and beautifully.

Newsletter
Add a real newsletter system to your blog. For free. With unlimited newsletters and subscribers.

Free Tools to Automate Your Site Growth
Free and easy way to double your email subscribers, plus sharing tools to double your traffic.

Easy WP SMTP
Easily send emails from your WordPress blog using your preferred SMTP server

Postman SMTP Mailer/Email Log
Postman is a next-generation SMTP Mailer, software that assists in the delivery of email generated content.

Genesis eNews Extended
Creates a new widget to easily add mailing lists integration to a Genesis website.

Email Address Encoder

A lightweight plugin to protect email addresses from email-harvesting robots by encoding them into decimal.

Email Subscribers & Newsletters

Add subscription forms on website, send HTML newsletters & automatically notify subscribers about new blog.

WP SMTP

WP SMTP can help us to send emails via SMTP instead of the PHP mail().

Configure SMTP

Configure SMTP mailing in WordPress, including support for sending e-mail via
SSL/TLS (such as GMail).

MailChimp Forms by MailMunch

MailChimp Forms to get more email subscribers.

SendGrid

Send emails and upload contacts through SendGrid from your WordPress installation using SMTP or API.

Easy Forms for MailChimp

The ultimate MailChimp WordPress plugin. Easily build unlimited forms for your MailChimp lists, add them.

Contact Form 7 MailChimp Extension

Simple way to integrate MailChimp mailing lists to Contact Form 7. Save your subscribers in…

Mail Bank – PHP Mail & SMTP Plugin
Mail Bank reconfigures the Mail Function and provides sophisticated SMTP settings to send and log...

WP Subscribe
WP Subscribe is a simple but powerful subscription plugin which supports MailChimp, Aweber and Feedburner.

wpMandrill
The wpMandrill plugin sends emails that are generated by WordPress through Mandrill, a transactional email...

Newsletter Sign-Up
Integrate your WordPress site with 3rd-party newsletter services like Aweber and YMLP. Adds various sign-up...

Form Builder & Popups Plugins (15)

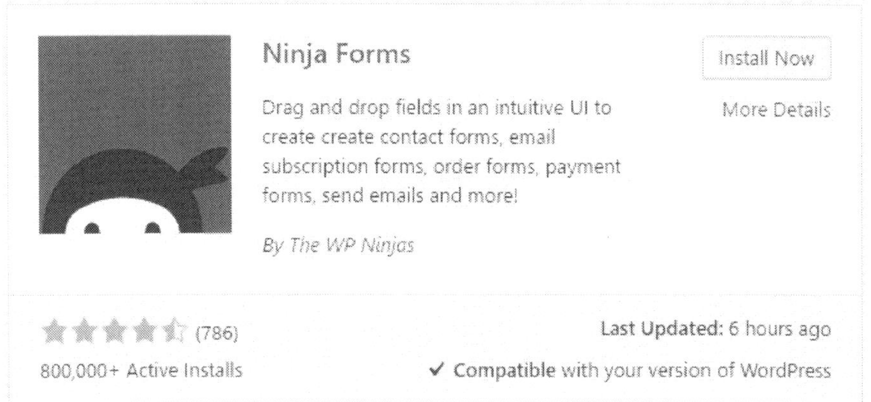

Ninja Forms
Ninja Forms is the ultimate free form creation tool for WordPress. Build forms within minutes using a simple yet powerful drag-and-drop form creator.

OptinMonster – Best WordPress Popup and Lead Generation Plugin
OptinMonster helps you grow your email list by converting visitors into subscribers and customers.

Formidable Forms
The best WordPress form plugin.

amoForms
Create forms and manage submissions easily with a simple interface.

Form Maker by WD – user-friendly drag & drop Form Builder plugin. Form Maker is a fresh and innovative form builder.

Form Builder
Form Builder is an intuitive tool for creating contact forms rearranging and editing fields.

Hustle – Pop-Ups, Slide-ins and Email Opt-ins
The complete marketing plugin for email opt-ins, pop-up advertising and building your user base.

Caldera Forms – More Than Contact Forms
Responsive form builder for contact forms, user registration and login forms, Mailchimp, and more.

Web-Settler Forms – Create Responsive Contact Forms
Contact form saves your hours of precious time by making contact form creation process super…

Popup
Popup Builder is the most complete pop up plugin. Html, image, shortcode and many other

Popups – WordPress Popup
Most complete free Popups plugin, scroll triggered popups, compatible with social networks, Gravity Forms, Ninja…

Forms – Form builder and Contact form
Form builder are one of the most important elements of your website. If you need…

Popups, Welcome Bar, Optins and Lead Generation Plugin – Icegram
Grow your subscriber list, engage and convert visitors, decrease bounce rate with this best in…

Easy Modal
The #1 WordPress Popup Plugin! Make glorious & powerful popups and market your content like…

Popup Maker
Create any popup imaginable! Customize your popups from head-to-toe and give your site more utility.

Favicon (3)

All In One Favicon
Easily add a Favicon to your site and the WordPress admin pages.

Favicon by RealFaviconGenerator
Generate and setup a favicon for desktop browsers, iPhone/iPad, Android devices, Windows 8 tablets, and more.

Favicon Rotator
Easily set site favicon and even rotate through multiple icons

Font Plugins (7)

Easy Google Fonts
Adds google fonts to any theme without coding and integrates with the WordPress Customizer automatically.

WP Google Fonts
The WP Google Fonts plugin allows you to easily add fonts from the Google Font palette.

Use Any Font
Embed any font in your website.

Disable Google Fonts
Disable enqueuing of Open Sans and other fonts used by WordPress from Google.

Font – official webfonts plugin of Fonts For Web. NO CODING! Just click & change font size, color and font face visually!
Finally official* web fonts plugin for WordPress. CLICK ON ANYTHING TO CHANGE IT(see screenshots)! Then…

WP SVG Icons
Quickly and effortlessly enable 490+ beautifully designed SVG font icons, available on the frontend and…

Styles
Be creative with colors and fonts. Styles changes everything.

Google Related Plugins (5)

Google Doc Embedder
Let's you embed PDF, MS Office, and many other file types in a web page.

Use Google Libraries
Allows your site to use common JavaScript libraries from Google's AJAX Libraries CDN.

DuracellTomi's Google Tag Manager for WordPress
The first Google Tag Manager plugin for WordPress with business goals in mind.

Verify Google Webmaster Tools
Adds Google Webmaster Tools verification meta tag and gets account verified.

Google Authenticator
Google Authenticator for your WordPress blog.

Image & Media Plugins (53)

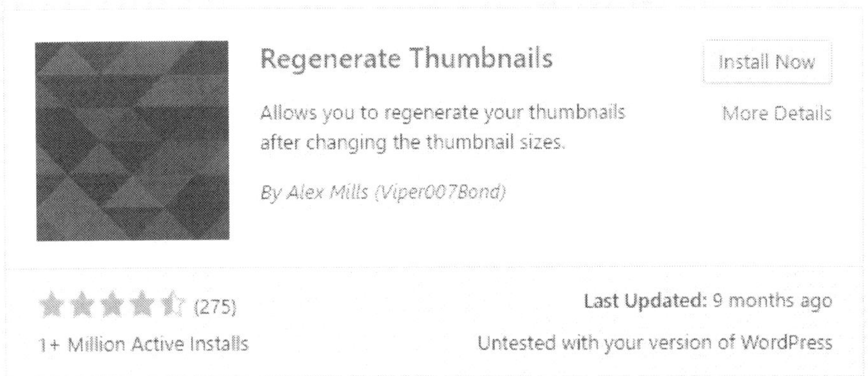

Regenerate Thumbnails
Allows you to regenerate your thumbnails after changing the thumbnail sizes.

Force Regenerate Thumbnails
Delete and REALLY force the regenerate thumbnail.

Image Widget
Image Widget is a simple plugin that uses the native WordPress media manager to add image widgets to your site.

EWWW Image Optimizer
Reduce image sizes in WordPress including NextGEN, GRAND FlAGallery, FooGallery and more using lossless/lossy methods.

Photo Gallery by WD – Responsive Photo Gallery for WordPress
Photo Gallery is an advanced plugin with a list of tools and options for adding photos.

Easy FancyBox
Easily enable the FancyBox jQuery extension on just about all media links.

Responsive Lightbox by dFactory
Responsive Lightbox allows users to view larger versions of images and galleries in a lightbox.

Enable Media Replace
This plugin allows you to replace a file in your media library by uploading a new file in its place.

Imsanity
Imsanity automatically resizes huge image uploads.

Simple Lightbox
The highly customizable lightbox for WordPress.

Auto Post Thumbnail
Automatically generate the Post Thumbnail (Featured Thumbnail) from the first image in post.

WP Lightbox 2
WP Lightbox 2 is awesome tool for adding responsive lightbox effect for images.

iframe
Speedup and protect WordPress in a smart way.

Video Thumbnails
Video Thumbnails simplifies the process of automatically displaying video thumbnails in your WordPress template.

AJAX Thumbnail Rebuild
AJAX Thumbnail Rebuild allows you to rebuild all thumbnails at once without script timeouts on your site.

FancyBox for WordPress
Seamlessly integrates FancyBox into your blog: Upload, activate, and you're done. Additional configuration optional.

Enhanced Media Library
A better management for WordPress Media Library.

WP jQuery Lightbox
A drop-in replacement for Lightbox 2 and similar plugins.

Gallery – Photo Gallery
Gallery image is the best gallery plugin to use if you want to be original.

Add From Server
"Add From Server" is a quick plugin which allows you to import media & files.

Simple Image Sizes
This plugin allow create custom image sizes for your site. Override your theme sizes directly.

Gallery by Envira – Responsive Photo Gallery for WordPress
The best WordPress gallery plugin. Drag & Drop photo gallery builder that helps you create.

Foo Gallery
Foo Gallery is the most intuitive and extensible gallery management tool ever created for WordPress.

WordPress Button Plugin MaxButtons
WordPress button plugin so powerful and easy to use anyone can create beautiful buttons and.

SVG Support
Allow SVG file uploads using the WordPress Media Library uploader plus direct styling/animation of SVG.

Dynamic Featured Image
Dynamically adds multiple featured image (post thumbnail) functionality to posts, pages and custom post types.

jQuery Colorbox
Adds Colorbox/Lightbox functionality to images, grouped by post or page. Works for WordPress and NextGEN.

Get the Image
An easy-to-use image script for adding things such as thumbnail, slider, gallery, and feature images.

Lightbox
Lightbox is the perfect tool for viewing photos.

Multiple Post Thumbnails
Adds multiple post thumbnails to a post type. If you've ever wanted more than one.

Photo Gallery by Supsystic
Photo Gallery with visual editor to build amazing photo gallery.

Advanced Responsive Video Embedder
Easy responsive video embeds via URLs or shortcodes. Perfect drop-in replacement for WordPress' default embeds.

Better Font Awesome
The Better Font Awesome plugin for WordPress. Shortcodes, HTML, TinyMCE, various Font Awesome versions, backwards.

WP Gallery Custom Links
Specify custom links for WordPress gallery images (instead of attachment or file only).

Gallery – Portfolio Gallery
Gallery – Portfolio Gallery is a great plugin for adding specialized portfolio galleriey, video portfolio.

Post Thumbnail Editor
Fed up with the lack of automated tools to properly crop and scale post thumbnails?

Imagify Image Optimizer
Dramatically reduce image file sizes without losing quality, make your website load faster, boost your.

Resize Image After Upload
Behind-the-scenes plugin to automatically resize images when uploaded, restricting size to within specified maximum h/w....

Menu Image
Adds a field to load the image in a menu item and displays the image...

WP Photo Album Plus
This plugin is designed to easily manage and display your photos, photo albums, slideshows and...

Media Library Assistant
Enhances the Media Library; powerful [mla_gallery] [mla_tag_cloud] [mla_term_list], taxonomy support, IPTC/EXIF/XMP/PDF processing, bulk/quick edit.

Slideshow Gallery
Feature content in a JavaScript powered slideshow gallery showcase on your WordPress website

Ultimate Responsive Image Slider
Add Fully Responsive Image Slider To Your WordPress Blog

Responsive Photo Gallery for WordPress by Gallery Bank
Gallery Bank is an advanced plugin which creates Beautiful Photo Galleries and Albums for different…

Gallery – Flagallery Photo Portfolio
Gallery Portfolio, Photo Gallery, Video Gallery, Music Album & Banner Rotator plugin with powerfull admin…

Video Embed & Thumbnail Generator
Makes video thumbnails, allows resolution switching, and embeds responsive self-hosted videos and galleries.

Image Watermark
Image Watermark allows you to automatically watermark images uploaded to the WordPress Media Library and…

Easy Watermark
Allows to add watermark to images automatically on upload or manually.

Optimus – WordPress Image Optimizer
Effective image compression and optimization during the upload process. Smart, automatic and reliable.

Tiled Gallery Carousel Without JetPack
Tiled Gallery Carousel allows you to display image galleries in mosaic styles without Jetpack.

Gallery – Photo Gallery and Images Gallery
Gallery modes photo gallery, images gallery, video gallery, Polaroid gallery, gallery lighbox, portfolio gallery, responsive…

Attachments
Attachments allows you to simply append any number of items from your WordPress Media Library…

Manual Image Crop
Plugin allows you to manually crop all the image sizes registered in your WordPress theme…

Language & Translation Plugins (9)

Loco Translate
Translate WordPress plugins and themes directly in your browser.

Polylang
Making WordPress multilingual.

Rus-To-Lat
Converts Cyrillic characters in post slugs to Latin characters.

qTranslate X
Adds a user-friendly multilingual dynamic content management.

Cyr to Lat enhanced
Converts Cyrillic, European and Georgian characters in post, page and term slugs to Latin characters.

Google Language Translator
Welcome to Google Language Translator! This plugin allows you to insert the Google Language Translator.

Translate WordPress with GTranslate
Translate WordPress with Google Translate multilanguage plugin to make your website multilingual.

Crayon Syntax Highlighter
Syntax Highlighter supporting multiple languages, themes, fonts, highlighting from a URL, or post text.

WPML Widgets
WPML Widgets is a simple to use extension to add a language selector dropdown to…

Login Plugins (11)

Nextend Facebook Connect
One click registration & login plugin for Facebook? Easy installation? Is it totally free.

Login With Ajax
Add smooth ajax login/registration effects and choose where users get redirected upon log in/out.

Sidebar Login
Easily add an ajax-enhanced login widget to your WordPress site sidebar.

WordPress Social Login
WordPress Social Login allow your visitors to comment and login with social networks such as.

Uber Login Logo
A simple, lightweight WordPress plugin to change your login logo.

Nextend Google Connect
One click registration & login plugin for Google? Easy installation? Is it totally free and…

Theme My Login
Themes the WordPress login pages according to your theme.

Social Login
Allow your visitors to comment and login with social networks like Twitter, Facebook, Paypal, LinkedIn,

Login Logo
Customize the logo on the WP login screen by simply dropping a file named login-logo.png.

Erident Custom Login and Dashboard
Customize completely your WordPress Login Screen easily. Add your logo, change background image, colors, styles,…

Add Logo to Admin
Add a custom logo to your wp-admin and login page.

Map Plugins (13)

WP Google Maps
The easiest to use Google maps plugin!

MapPress Easy Google Maps
MapPress is the most popular and easiest way to create great-looking
Google Maps.

Google Maps Widget
Tired of buggy and slow Google Maps plugins taking hours to setup?

Comprehensive Google Map Plugin
A simple and intuitive, yet elegant and fully documented Google map
plugin that installs as.

WP Google Map Plugin
A Google Maps plugin for WordPress to create unlimited locations,
maps and display google map.

Google Map
Google Map plugin form Huge-IT-the best solution to add awesome
Google Maps to your website.

API KEY for Google Maps
Retroactively add Google Maps API KEY to any theme or plugin.

WordPress Google Maps Plugin
A simple, easy and quite powerful Google Maps tool to create, manage and embed custom…

Leaflet Maps Marker (Google Maps, OpenStreetMap, Bing Maps)
The most comprehensive & user-friendly mapping solution for WordPress

Simple Map
Easy way to embed google map(s).

Visitor Maps and Who's Online
Displays Visitor Maps with location pins, city, and country. Includes a Who's Online Sidebar. Has…

Google Maps Easy
WordPress Google Maps

Maps Builder – Google Maps Plugin
The most flexible, robust, and easy to use WordPress plugin for creating powerful Google Maps…

Miscellaneous (27)

WP Multibyte Patch
Multibyte functionality enhancement for the WordPress Japanese package.

WP Job Manager
Manage job listings from the WordPress admin panel, and allow users to post job listings

Download Monitor
Download Monitor is a plugin for uploading and managing downloads, tracking downloads, and displaying links.

PDF Embedder
Embed PDFs straight into your posts and pages, with intelligent resizing of width and height.

Really Simple CSV Importer
Alternative CSV Importer plugin. Simple and powerful, best for geeks.

Import any XML or CSV File to WordPress
WP All Import is an extremely powerful importer that makes it easy to import any.

FeedWordPress
FeedWordPress syndicates content from feeds you choose into your WordPress weblog.

One Click Demo Import
Import your demo content, widgets and theme settings with one click. Theme authors! Enable simple demo import for your theme demo data.

Heartbeat Control
Allows you to easily manage the frequency of the WordPress heartbeat API.

PowerPress Podcasting plugin by Blubrry
No. 1 Podcasting plugin for WordPress, with simple & advanced modes, players, subscribe tools, and.

Disable Emojis
This plugin disables the new WordPress emoji functionality.

WP Total Hacks
WP Total Hacks can customize more than 20 settings on your WordPress Site. PHP5 is…

Easy Smooth Scroll Links
Create anchors and add up to to 30 scrolling animation effects to links that link…

SoundCloud Shortcode
SoundCloud Shortcode plugin for WordPress

No Self Pings
Keeps WordPress from sending pings to your own site.

Compact WP Audio Player
A Compact WP Audio Player Pluign that is compatible with all major browsers and devices…

WP RSS Aggregator
WP RSS Aggregator is the most comprehensive RSS feed importer and autoblogging plugin for WordPress…

Multi Device Switcher
This WordPress plugin allows you to set a separate theme for device (Smart Phone, Tablet...

WP-Print
Displays a printable version of your WordPress blog's post/page.

Logo Carousel
Show your partners, clients or sponsors on your website in a logo carousel!

Ditty News Ticker
Ditty News Ticker is a multi-functional data display plugin.

Gwolle Guestbook
Gwolle Guestbook is the WordPress guestbook you've just been looking for. Beautiful and easy.

Embed Any Document
Easiest way to upload and display PDF, MS Office and more documents on your WordPress...

MP3-jPlayer
Easy, Flexible Audio for WordPress.

WP Live Chat Support
Fully functional Live Chat plugin. Chat with your visitors for free! No need for monthly...

MediaElement.js – HTML5 Video & Audio Player
MediaElement.js is an HTML5 video and audio player with Flash fallback and captions. Supports IE,...

WordPress Ping Optimizer
Save your WordPress blog from getting tagged as ping spammer.

Polls, Rating, and Survey Plugins (8)

WP-Polls
Adds an AJAX poll system to your WordPress blog.

WP-PostRatings
Adds an AJAX rating system for your WordPress site's content.

WP Product Review Lite
Easily turn your basic posts into in-depth reviews with ratings, pros and cons, affiliate links.

WP Customer Reviews
Allows your visitors to leave business / product reviews.

Testimonials Widget
Easily add social proofing to your website with Testimonials Widget. List or slide reviews via.

kk Star Ratings
kk Star Ratings allows blog visitors to involve and interact more effectively with your website…

Testimonials Plugin: Easy Testimonials
Testimonials widget and shortcode for adding Testimonials to your WordPress Theme, with a simple interface.

Testimonial Rotator
Easily add Testimonials to your WordPress Blog or Company Website.

Popular, Recent, & Related Post Plugins (11)

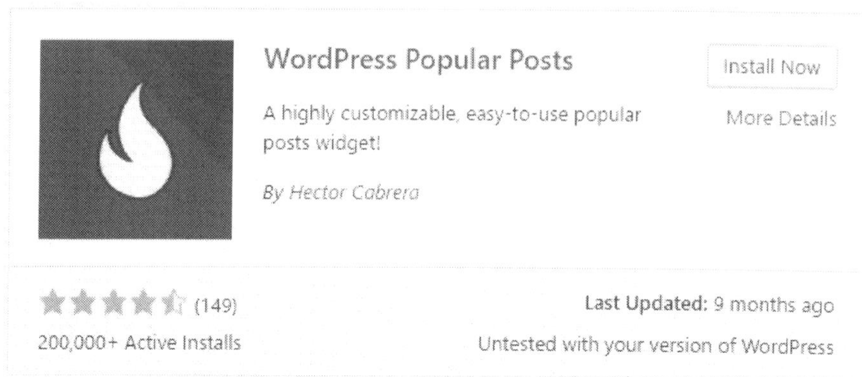

WordPress Popular Posts
A highly customizable, easy-to-use popular posts widget!

Yet Another Related Posts Plugin (YARPP)
Display a list of related posts on your site based on a powerful unique algorithm.

Recent Posts Widget Extended
Provides flexible and advanced recent posts.

WordPress Related Posts
WordPress Related Posts – the plugin for related posts with thumbnails. Caching included.

Recent Posts Widget With Thumbnails
List of your site's most recent posts, with clickable title and thumbnails.

Contextual Related Posts

Display related posts on your WordPress blog and feed. Supports thumbnails, shortcodes, widgets and custom.

Similar Posts – Powerful Related Posts Plugin
Displays a list of related posts similar to the current one based on content, title.

Related Posts
Link to related content to help your readers. Get attention from other authors. Make great…

Related Posts
Related posts a so easy and fast

Top 10 – Popular posts plugin for WordPress
Track daily and total visits on your blog posts. Display the count as well as…

Related Posts
Related Posts is The Best Customizable plugin, that nicely displays related posts thumbnails under the…

Redirection & Link Management Plugins (24)

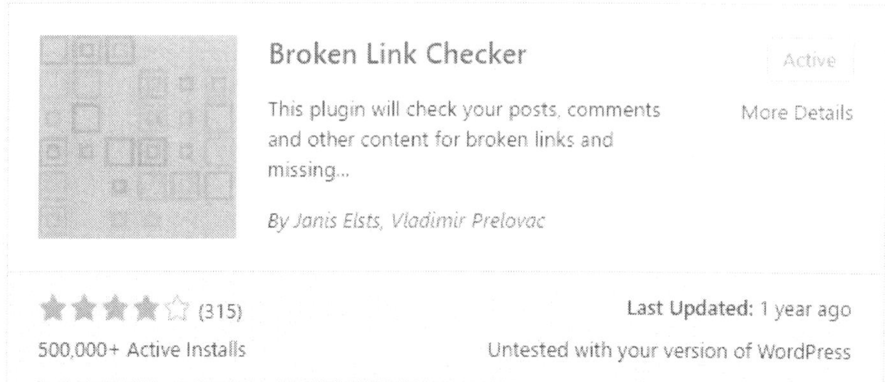

Broken Link Checker

This plugin will check your posts, comments and other content for broken links and missing links.

Redirection

Redirection is a WordPress plugin to manage 301 redirections and keep track of 404 errors.

Page Links To

This plugin allows you to make a WordPress page or post link to a URL of your choosing, instead of its WordPress page or post URL.

Quick Page/Post Redirect Plugin

Easily redirect pages/posts or custom post types to another page/post or external URL.

Simple 301 Redirects

Simple 301 Redirects provides an easy method of redirecting requests to another page on your site.

Pretty Link Lite
Shrink, beautify, track, manage and share any URL on or off your WordPress website.

Link Manager
Enables the Link Manager that existed in WordPress until version 3.5.

Velvet Blues Update URLs
Updates all URLs and content links in your website.

All 404 Redirect to Homepage
By using this smart plugin, you can fix all 404-error links by redirecting them.

Custom Permalinks
Set custom permalinks on a per-post, per-tag or per-category basis.

404 to 301
Automatically redirect, log and notify all 404 page errors to any page using 301 redirect.

Custom Post Type Permalinks
Edit the permalink of custom post type.

No Category Base (WPML)
This plugin removes the mandatory 'Category Base' from your category permalinks.

.html on PAGES
Appends .html to the URL of PAGES when using permalinks.

404 Redirection
Permanently redirect all 404's to the main blog URL. The primary purpose is to salvage.

404 to Start
Send 404 page not found error directly to start page (or any other page/site) to.

SEO Redirection Plugin
SEO Redirection is a the best plugin to manage 301 redirections without requiring knowledge of.

Eggplant 301 Redirects
Easily manage and create 301 redirects for your WordPress website.

Remove Category URL
This plugin removes '/category' from your category permalinks. (e.g. /category/my-category/ to /my-category/)

Safe Redirect Manager
Safely and easily manage your website's HTTP redirects.

Open external links in a new window
Opens all (or specific) external links in a new window. XHTML Strict compliant and search…

External Links
The external links plugin for WordPress lets you process outgoing links differently from internal links.

404page – your smart custom 404 error page
Custom 404 the easy way! Set any page as custom 404 error page. No coding…

Go Live Update URLS
Goes through entire site and replaces all instances of and old url with a new…

Security Plugins (35)

Jetpack by WordPress.com
Keep any WordPress site secure, increase traffic, and engage your readers.

Limit Login Attempts
Limit rate of login attempts, including by way of cookies, for each IP. Fully customizable.

Wordfence Security
Secure your website with the most comprehensive WordPress security plugin.

iThemes Security (formerly Better WP Security)
iThemes Security is the #1 WordPress Security Plugin.

All in One WP Security & Firewall
A comprehensive, user-friendly, all in one WordPress security and firewall plugin for your site.

Loginizer
Loginizer is a WordPress security plugin which helps you fight against bruteforce attacks.

Sucuri Security – Auditing, Malware Scanner and Security Hardening
The Sucuri WordPress Security plugin is a toolset for security integrity monitoring, malware detection, and more.

MainWP Child
Provides a secure connection between your MainWP Dashboard and your WordPress sites.

Login LockDown
Limits the number of login attempts from a given IP range within a certain time.

Anti-Malware Security and Brute-Force Firewall
This Anti-Malware scanner searches for Malware, Viruses, and other security threats and vulnerabilities on your website.

Really Simple SSL
No setup required! You only need an SSL certificate, and this plugin will do the rest.

Rename wp-login.php
Change wp-login.php to anything you want.

Password Protected
A very simple way to quickly password protect your WordPress site with a single password.

WPS Hide Login
Change wp-login.php to anything you want.

BulletProof Security
Secure WordPress Website Security Protection: Firewall Security, Login Security, Database Security & Backup.

AntiVirus
Security plugin to protect your blog or website against exploits and spam injections.

WordPress HTTPS (SSL)
WordPress HTTPS is intended to be an all-in-one solution to using SSL on WordPress sites.

Theme Authenticity Checker
Scan all of your theme files for potentially malicious or unwanted code.

SSL Insecure Content Fixer
Clean up WordPress website HTTPS insecure content.

Peter's Login Redirect
Redirect users to different locations after logging in and logging out.

BBQ: Block Bad Queries
The fastest firewall plugin for WordPress.

Custom Login Page Customizer
Custom Login Customizer allows you to easily customize your admin login page, straight from your.

Acunetix Secure WordPress
plugins, private, protection, tracking, WordPress Requires at least: 3.0 Tested up to: 4.2 Stable tag

Timthumb Vulnerability Scanner
Scans your wp-content directory for vulnerable instances of timthumb.php, and optionally upgrades them to a.

WP Content Copy Protection & No Right Click
This wp plugin protect the posts content from being copied by any other web site.

Shield Security
Protect your website, your reputation, and your customers for free with Shield Security, the most.

WP Security Audit Log
Keep an audit trail of all changes and under the hood WordPress activity to ensure…

WP-CopyProtect [Protect your blog posts]
Protect your blog content from getting copied. A simple plug-in developed to stop the Copy…

Login Logout Menu
You can now add a correct login & logout link in your WP menus.

VaultPress
VaultPress is a subscription service offering real-time backup, automated security scanning, and support from WordPress…

WP Content Copy Protection

WP Content Copy Protection uses aggressive techniques in protecting your online content (text/source/images/video/audio) from being...

CloudFlare Flexible SSL

Fix For CloudFlare Flexible SSL Redirect Loop For WordPress.

WP Limit Login Attempts

Limit Login Attempts for login protection. Limit rate of login attempts and block IP temporarily....

BruteProtect

BruteProtect is no longer actively supported. All new development is now being done on the...

WP fail2ban

Write a myriad of WordPress events to syslog for integration with fail2ban.

SEO & Search Plugins (15)

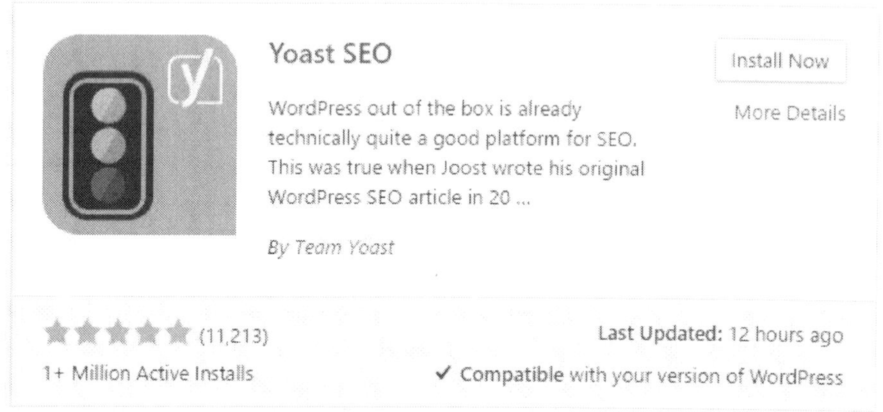

Yoast SEO
WordPress out of the box is already technically quite a good platform for SEO.

All in One SEO Pack
The original SEO plugin for WordPress, downloaded over 30,000,000 times since 2007.

Meta Slider
The most popular WordPress slider plugin. Creating slideshows with Meta Slider is fast and easy. Simply select images from your WordPress Media Library, drag and drop them into place, set slide captions, links and SEO fields all from one page.

SEO Ultimate
This all-in-one SEO plugin gives you control over meta titles & descriptions, open graph, auto-linking, and more.

Add Meta Tags
A metadata plugin that can optimize your web site for more efficient indexing and easier.

Search & Replace
Search & Replace data in your database with WordPress admin, replace domains/URLs of your WordPress.

Relevanssi – A Better Search
Relevanssi replaces the default search with a partial-match search that sorts results by relevance.

Search Everything
Search Everything increases WordPress' default search functionality in three easy steps.

Search Regex
Search Regex adds a powerful set of search and replace functions to WordPress that go.

All In One Schema.org Rich Snippets
Boost CTR. Improve SEO & Rankings. Supports most of the content type. Works perfectly with.

Facebook Open Graph, Google+ and Twitter Card Tags
Inserts Facebook Open Graph, Google+/Schema.org, Twitter and SEO Meta Tags into your WordPress Website for.

SEO by SQUIRRLY™
SEO Plugin By Squirrly is for the NON-SEO experts. Get Excellent SEO with Better Content,…

WP External Links (nofollow new tab seo)
Open external links in a new tab / window, add "nofollow", "noopener" and font icons,…

Glue for Yoast SEO & AMP
This plugin makes sure the default WordPress AMP plugin uses the proper Yoast SEO metadata…

Better Search Replace
A simple plugin to update URLs or other text in a database.

Shortcode & Code Plugins (9)

Shortcodes Ultimate
Supercharge your WordPress theme with mega pack of shortcodes.

Display Posts Shortcode
Display a listing of posts using the [display-posts] shortcode.

Easy Bootstrap Shortcode
Easy Bootstrap Shortcode enable you to add bootstrap 3.0.3 styles in your pages, post and…

Bootstrap Shortcodes for WordPress
Implements Bootstrap 3 styles and components in WordPress through shortcodes.

Posts in Page
Easily add one or more posts to any page using simple shortcodes.

Code Snippets
An easy, clean and simple way to add code snippets to your site.

Shortcodes by Angie Makes
A plugin that adds a useful family of shortcodes to your WordPress theme.

Column Shortcodes
Adds shortcodes to easily create columns in your posts or pages.

Raw HTML
Lets you use raw HTML or any other code in your posts. You can also…

Site Administration Plugins (81)

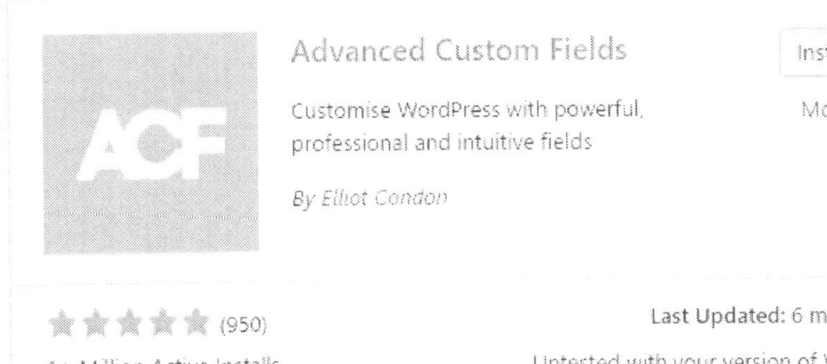

Advanced Custom Fields
Customize WordPress with powerful, professional and intuitive fields.

WP-PageNavi
Adds a more advanced paging navigation interface.

WP-Optimize
WP-Optimize is an effective tool for automatically cleaning your WordPress database so that it runs at maximum efficiency.

Post Types Order
A powerful plugin, Order Posts and Post Types Objects using a Drag and Drop Sortable JavaScript capability.

Custom Post Type UI
Admin UI for creating custom post types and custom taxonomies for WordPress.

InfiniteWP Client
Install this plugin on unlimited sites and manage them all from a central dashboard.

ManageWP Worker

ManageWP is the ultimate WordPress productivity tool, allowing you to efficiently manage your websites.

All-in-One WP Migration

All-in-One WP Migration is the only tool that you will ever need to migrate a website.

WP Clone by WP Academy

Move or copy a WordPress site to another server or to another domain name, move, and more.

Simple Page Ordering

Order your pages and other hierarchical post types with simple drag and drop.

Toolset Types

The complete and reliable plugin for managing custom post types, custom taxonomies and custom fields.

Category Order and Taxonomy Terms Order

Order Categories and all custom taxonomies terms (hierarchically) and child terms using a drag and drop.

Meta Box

Meta Box plugin is a powerful, professional developer toolkit to create custom meta boxes.

Exclude Pages

This plugin adds a checkbox, "include this page in menus", uncheck this to exclude pages.

WP Migrate DB

Migrates your database by running find & replace on URLs and file paths, handling serialized.

Admin Menu Editor
Let's you edit the WordPress admin menu.

Insert Headers and Footers
This plugin allows you to add extra scripts to the header and footer of your site.

Adminimize
Adminimize that lets you hide 'unnecessary' items from the WordPress backend.

SG Optimizer
The SG Optimizer is designed to link WordPress with all SiteGround Performance services.

Intuitive Custom Post Order
Intuitively, order items (Posts, Pages, and Custom Post Types, and Custom Taxonomies) using a drag and drop sortable JavaScript.

WP-DBManager
Manages your WordPress database.

Easy Theme and Plugin Upgrades
Easily upgrade your themes and plugins using zip files without removing the theme or plugin.

WP Editor
WP Editor is a plugin for WordPress that replaces the default plugin and theme editors.

Max Mega Menu
An easy to use mega menu plugin. Written the WordPress way.

Simple Custom Post Order
Order posts (posts, any custom post types) using a Drag and Drop Sortable JavaScript.

Theme Check
A simple and easy way to test your theme for all the latest WordPress standards.

White Label CMS
Customize dashboard panels and branding, remove menus, give editors access to widgets plus lots more.

Options Framework
The Options Framework Plugin makes it easy to include an options panel in any WordPress.

Head, Footer and Post Injections
Header and Footer plugin let you to add html code to the head and footer.

Easy Updates Manager
Manage all your WordPress updates, including individual updates, automatic updates, logs, and loads more.

CMB2
CMB2 is a metabox, custom fields, and forms library for WordPress that will blow your mind.

Post Duplicator
Creates functionality to duplicate any and all post types, including taxonomies & custom fields.

Revision Control

Revision Control allows finer control over the Post Revision system included with WordPress.

Advanced Code Editor

Enables syntax highlighting in the integrated themes and plugins source code editors with line numbers.

Menu Icons

Spice up your navigation menus with pretty icons, easily.

Advanced Automatic Updates

Adds extra options to WordPress' built-in Automatic Updates feature.

Category Order

The Order Categories plugin allows you to easily reorder your categories the way you want.

Portfolio Post Type

This plugin registers a custom post type for portfolio items.

CMS Tree Page View

Adds a tree view of all pages & custom posts.

Reveal IDs

What this plugin does is to reveal most removed IDs on admin pages, as it.

WordPress Database Reset

A plugin that allows you to skip the 5 minute installation and reset WordPress's database.

Optimize Database after Deleting Revisions

This plugin is a 'One Click' WordPress Database Cleaner / Optimizer.

Admin Columns
Manage and organize columns in the posts, users, comments and media lists in the WordPress admin panel.

Categories Images
The Categories Images Plugin allow you to add image with category or taxonomy.

WP Robots Txt
WP Robots Txt Allows you to edit the content of your robots.txt file.

Disable XML-RPC Pingback
Stops abuse of your site's XML-RPC by simply removing some methods used by attackers.

Disable XML-RPC
This plugin disables XML-RPC API in WordPress 3.5+, which is enabled by default.

Better Delete Revision
Better Delete Revision not only deletes redundant revisions of posts from your WordPress Database, it.

WP-Paginate
WP-Paginate is a simple and flexible pagination plugin which provides users with better navigation on.

Categories to Tags Converter
Convert existing categories to tags or tags to categories, selectively.

The WP Remote WordPress Plugin
WP Remote is a free web app that enables you to easily manage all of.

Post Grid, List for WordPress – Content Views
Display recent or any posts by category, tag, author, ID in responsive grid, list layout.

Bulk Delete
Bulk delete posts, pages, users, attachments and meta fields based on different conditions and filters.

WP Clean Up
WP Clean Up can help us to clean up the WordPress database by removing "revision"

WP Hide Post
Enables you to control the visibility of items on your blog by making posts/pages hidden.

Activity Log
The #1 Activity Log plugin helps you monitor & log all changes and activities on.

PHP Code for posts
Add PHP code to your WordPress posts, pages, custom post types and even sidebars using…

WP Crontrol
WP Crontrol lets you view and control what's happening in the WP-Cron system.

SyntaxHighlighter Evolved
Easily post syntax-highlighted code to your site without having to modify the code at all.…

Capability Manager Enhanced
A simple way to manage WordPress roles and capabilities.

Customizer Export/Import
Easily export or import your WordPress customizer settings!

Post Type Archive Link
Creates a metabox to the Appearance > Menu page to add custom post type archive…

WP Htaccess Editor
Simple editor htaccess file without using FTP client.

WordPress REST API (Version 2)
Access your site's data through an easy-to-use HTTP REST API. (Version 2)

jQuery Updater
This plugin updates jQuery to the latest stable version on your website.

SSH SFTP Updater Support
"SSH SFTP Updater Support" is the easiest way to keep your WordPress installation up-to-date with…

WP Updates Notifier
Sends email to notify you if there are any updates for your WordPress site.

WP-Sweep
WP-Sweep allows you to clean up unused, orphaned and duplicated data in your WordPress. It…

AG Custom Admin
All-in-one tool for admin panel customization. Change almost everything: admin menu, dashboard, login page, admin…

WP Admin UI Customize
Customize the management screen UI.

Ultimate Nofollow
Adds a checkbox in the insert link popup box for including rel="nofollow" in links as...

Custom Field Suite
A custom fields management UI

Menu Social Icons
Add social icons to your WordPress menu items automatically.

Ultimate Category Excluder
Ultimate Category Excluder allows you to quickly and easily exclude categories from your front page,...

Debug Bar
Adds a debug menu to the admin bar that shows query, cache, and other helpful...

Meta Tag Manager
Easily add and manage custom meta tags to various parts of your site or on...

File Manager
File Manager provides you ability to edit, delete, upload, download, copy and paste files and...

Admin Menu Tree Page View
Get a tree view of all your pages directly in the admin menu. Search, edit,...

Calculated Fields Form
Calculated Fields Form is a plugin for creating forms with dynamically calculated fields and display...

Post Tags and Categories for Pages
Adds the built in WordPress categories and tags to your pages.

WP-Memory-Usage
Show up the PHP version, memory limit and current memory usage in the dashboard and...

Site Unavailable & Under Construction Plugins (10)

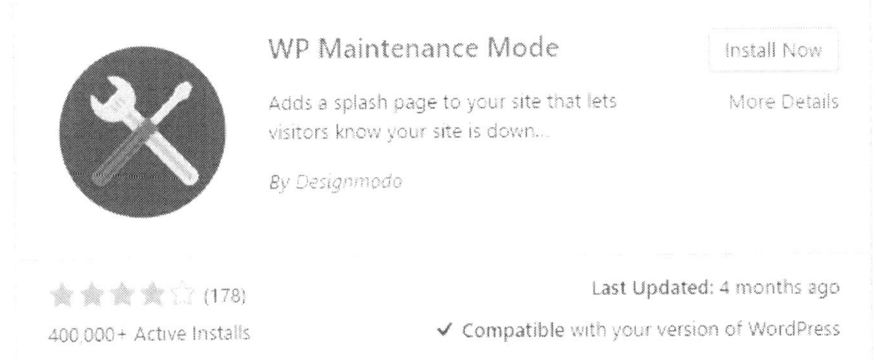

WP Maintenance Mode
Adds a splash page to your site that lets visitors know your site is down.

Maintenance
Maintenance plugin allow WordPress site administrator close the website for maintenance, enable "503 Service temporarily unavailable", set a temporary page with authorization, which can be edited via the plugin settings.

Coming Soon Page & Maintenance Mode by SeedProd
The #1 Coming Soon Page, Under Construction & Maintenance Mode plugin for WordPress.

underConstruction
Creates a 'Coming Soon' page that will show for all users who are not logged in.

Ultimate Coming Soon Page
Creates a Coming Soon page or Launch page for your Website while it's under construction.

Under Construction / Maintenance Mode from Acurax
The easiest and feature-rich plugin to show under construction, coming soon, maintenance mode to visitors.

Under Construction
Display an Under Construction, Maintenance Mode or Landing Page that takes 5 seconds to setup.

Maintenance Mode
Maintenance mode with progress bar and responsive layout. Adds a responsive maintenance mode page to

Maintenance Mode
Very simple Maintenance Mode & Coming soon page using default WordPress markup with no ads…

Coming soon, Maintenance Mode, Under Construction
Coming soon and Maintenance mode plugin is an awesome tool to show your website visitors…

Sitemap Plugins (11)

Google XML Sitemaps
This plugin will generate a special XML sitemap which will help search engines like Google, Bing, Yahoo and Ask.com to better index your blog.

PS Auto Sitemap
Auto generator of a customizable and designed sitemap page.

Better WordPress Google XML Sitemaps (support Sitemap Index, Multi-site and Google News)
A WordPress XML Sitemap plugin that comes with support for Sitemap Index, Multi-site and Google.

WP Sitemap Page
Add a sitemap on any of your page using the simple shortcode [wp_sitemap_page].

XML Sitemap & Google News feeds
XML and Google News Sitemaps to feed the hungry spiders. Multisite, WP Super Cache, and Polylang.

Google Sitemap by BestWebSoft

Generate and add XML sitemap to WordPress website. Help search engines index your blog.

Google XML Sitemap for Videos

This plugin will help you generate Google Video Sitemaps (XML) for your WordPress blog.

Simple Sitemap

The simplest responsive HTML sitemap available for WordPress! No setup required. Flexible customization options available.

HTML Page Sitemap

Adds an HTML (Not XML) sitemap of your pages (not posts) by entering the shortcode...

WP Realtime Sitemap

A sitemap plugin to make it easier for your site to show all your pages,

Simple Wp Sitemap

An easy sitemap plugin that adds both an xml and an html sitemap to your...

Slider Plugins (9)

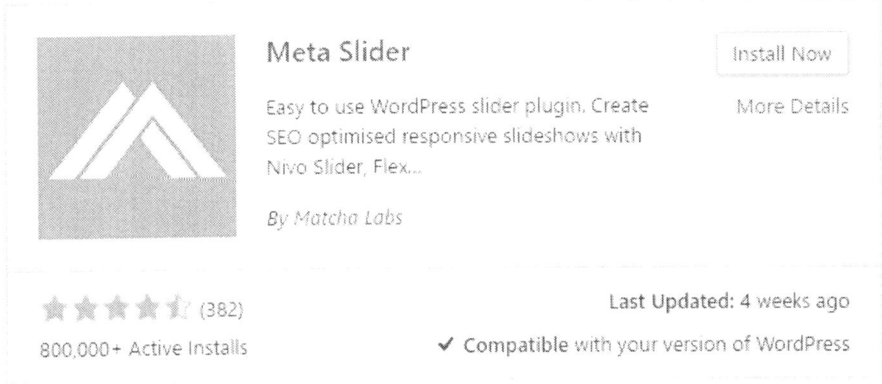

Meta Slider
The most popular WordPress slider plugin. Creating slideshows with Meta Slider is fast and easy. Simply select images from your WordPress Media Library, drag and drop them into place, set slide captions, links and SEO fields all from one page.

Slider – Image Slider
Slider Huge-IT is an awesome WordPress Slider Plugin with many nice features.

Master Slider – Responsive Touch Slider
The most advanced responsive and HTML5 WordPress slider plugin with touch swipe navigation that works.

Slider by Soliloquy – Responsive Image Slider for WordPress
The best WordPress slider plugin. Drag & Drop responsive slider builder that helps you create.

Easing Slider
The easiest way to create sliders with WordPress.

Smart Slider 3

Responsive slider plugin to create beautiful sliders in the next generation visual editor.

Cyclone Slider 2

An easy-to-use and customizable slideshow plugin. For both casual users and expert developers.

Meteor Slides

Easily create responsive slideshows with WordPress that are mobile friendly and simple to customize.

Slider by WD – Responsive Slider for WordPress

Slider WD plugin is the perfect slider solution for WordPress.

Social Media & Sharing Plugins (42)

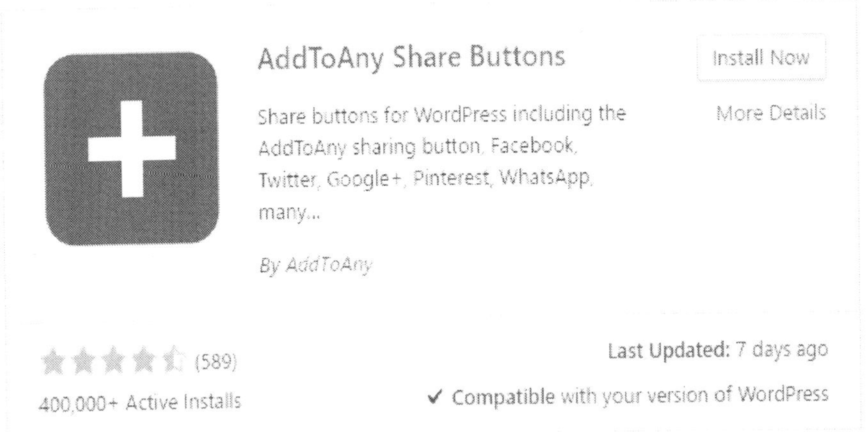

AddToAny Share Buttons
Share buttons for WordPress including the AddToAny sharing button, Facebook, Twitter, Google+, Pinterest, WhatsApp, and many more.

Instagram Feed
Display beautifully clean, customizable, and responsive feeds from multiple Instagram accounts.

Simple Social Icons
This plugin allows you to insert social icons in any widget area.

Share Buttons by AddThis
Increase social traffic to your website with WordPress share buttons.

Custom Facebook Feed
Display a completely customizable, responsive and search engine crawlable version of your Facebook feed on your website.

NextScripts: Social Networks Auto-Poster
Automatically publishes blogposts to profiles/pages/groups on Facebook, Twitter, Instagram, Google+, Pinterest, LinkedIn, Blogger, Tumblr, and more.

Social Media Widget
Adds links to all of your social media and sharing site profiles.

Free Tools to Automate Your Site Growth
Free and easy way to double your email subscribers, plus sharing tools to double your traffic.

WP Instagram Widget
WP Instagram widget is a no fuss WordPress widget to showcase your latest Instagram pics.

Simple Share Buttons Adder
A simple plugin that enables you to add share buttons to all of your posts.

Social Media Feather | social media sharing
Lightweight, modern looking and effective social media sharing and profile buttons and icons.

Shareaholic | share buttons, related posts, social analytics & more
World's leading all-in-one Content Amplification Platform that helps grow your site traffic, engagement, conversions & more.

Facebook Like Box Widget
Facebook Like Box Widget is a social plugin that enables Facebook Page owners to attract.

Easy Facebook Like Box – Custom Facebook Feed – Auto PopUp
Easy Facebook like box WordPress plugin allows to display custom Facebook feed.

oAuth Twitter Feed for Developers
Twitter API 1.1 compliant plugin that provides a function to get an array of tweet.

Facebook Widget
This widget adds a Simple Facebook page Like Widget into your WordPress website Sidebar.

Social Share WordPress Plugin – AccessPress Social Share
Share your site urls in most popular social medias and show share counts on your.

Instagram Slider Widget
Instagram Slider Widget is a responsive slider widget that shows 12 latest images from a.

Social Icons WordPress Plugin – AccessPress Social Icons
Add social media icons on your site | select from pre-designed sets or upload your.

Social Media and Share Icons (Ultimate Social Media)
Easy to use social media plugin which adds social media icons to your website with.

WP to Twitter
Posts a Twitter update when you update your WordPress blog or add a link.

Instagram Feed WD – Instagram Gallery for WordPress
Instagram Feed WD is a user-friendly plugin to display user or hashtag-based Instagram feeds as.

Facebook Conversion Pixel
In 2016, Facebook transitioned to an updated version of the Custom Audience and Conversion pixels.

Facebook
Facebook Like Box plugin comes with Facebook Like Box Widget & Shortcode.

Social Media
Super-easy to use social media plugin which adds social media icons to your website with.

Social Media Share Buttons | MashShare
Social Media Share Buttons for Twitter, Facebook and other social networks.

Tracking Code Manager
A plugin to manage ALL your tracking code and conversion pixels.

Social Media Flying Icons | Floating Social Media Icon
Social Media Plugin with 30+ Social Media Icon Styles,Easy Configuration,Social Media Widget,Icon Animation,Drag Reorder,Highly Customizable.

Social Counter for WordPress – AccessPress Social Counter
A plugin to display your social accounts fans, subscribers and followers number on your website.

Facebook Like Box
Facebook like box plugin will help you to display Facebook like box on your wesite,

Feed Them Social – Facebook, Instagram, Twitter, Vine, Pinterest, etc
Custom feeds for Facebook Pages, Groups, Events, Album Photos, Videos & Covers, Twitter, Vine, Instagram,…

Easy Social Icons
Upload your own social media icons or choose from font-awesome. Use widget|shortcode to place icons…

Social Count Plus
Displays your number of followers from Facebook, Google+, Instagram, Twitch, Twitter and several other social…

Facebook Pixel by PixelYourSite – Events, WooCommerce & Easy Digital Downloads
Insert the new Facebook Pixel on WordPress, add Events, enjoy superb WooCommerce & EDD Facebook…

I Recommend This
This plugin allows your visitors to simply like/recommend your posts instead of comment on it.

Social Share Buttons – Social Pug
Social share buttons with style that will increase your social shares and user interaction with…

Social Media Widget by Acurax
Social Media Widget Plugin, A Simple Social Icon Widget To Show Essential Social Media Icons…

Facebook Auto Publish
Publish posts automatically to Facebook page or profile.

Lightweight Social Icons
Looking to add simple social icons to your widget areas? Choose the size and color...

Facebook Button by BestWebSoft
Add Facebook Follow, Like, and Share buttons to WordPress posts, pages, and widgets.

Rotating Tweets (Twitter widget and shortcode)
Twitter widget and shortcode to show your latest tweets one at a time an animated...

Pinterest Pin It Button On Image Hover And Post
Pin Your WordPress Blog Posts Pages Images With Pinterest Plugin

Table & Database Plugins (2)

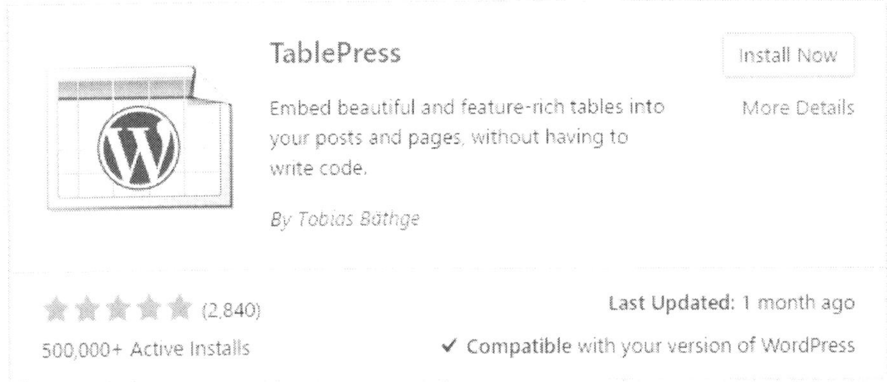

TablePress

Embed beautiful and feature-rich tables into your posts and pages, without having to write code.

Pricing Table Builder – Easy Pricing Tables

Pricing Table Builder – Easy Pricing Tables Lets You Create A Beautiful, Responsive Pricing Table...

Terms, Site Info, and Cookie Plugins (8)

Cookie Notice by dFactory
Cookie Notice allows you to elegantly inform users that your site uses cookies.

Cookie Law Info
A simple way to show how your website complies with the EU Cookie Law.

Auto Terms of Service and Privacy Policy
Put your own details into a modified version of Automattic's "Terms of Service" and "Privacy Policy."

Cookie Consent
The only cookie consent plugin you'll ever need.

EU Cookie Law
EU Cookie Law informs users that your site uses cookies, with option to lock scripts.

Asesor de Cookies para normativa española
Este plugin le va a facilitar la confección de la política de cookies para.

Italy Cookie Choices (for EU Cookie Law)
Italy Cookie Choices allows you to easily comply with the european cookie law and block...

Cookies for Comments
Sets a cookie on a random URL that is then checked when a comment is...

User Management Plugins (10)

User Role Editor
User Role Editor WordPress plugin makes user roles and capabilities changing easy.

WP User Avatar
Use any image from your WordPress Media Library as a custom user avatar.

Nav Menu Roles
Hide custom menu items based on user roles.

WP-UserOnline
Enable you to display how many users are online on your WordPress blog with detailed...

Simple Local Avatars
Adds an avatar upload field to user profiles. Generates requested sizes on demand just like.

User Switching
Instant switching between user accounts in WordPress.

Edit Author Slug
Allows an admin (or capable user) to edit the author slug of a user, and.

WPFront User Role Editor
Easily allows you to manage WordPress user roles. You can create, edit, delete and manage.

User Access Manager
With the "User Access Manager"-plugin you can manage the access to your posts, pages and…

Remove Dashboard Access
Allows you to disable Dashboard access for users of a specific role or capability. Disallowed…

Visual Editor, Page Builder, CSS, & Theme Plugins (41)

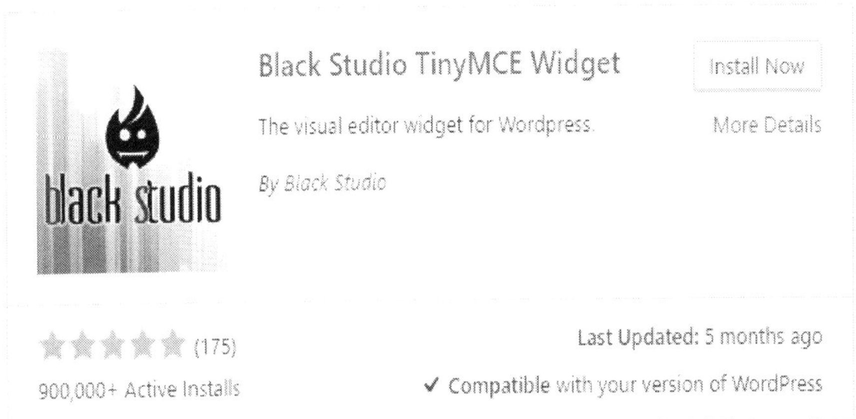

Black Studio TinyMCE Widget
The visual editor widget for WordPress.

TinyMCE Advanced
Extends and enhances TinyMCE, the WordPress Visual Editor.

Redux Framework
Redux is a simple, truly extensible and fully responsive options framework for WordPress themes.

Genesis Simple Edits
This plugin creates a new Genesis settings page that allows you to modify the post-info (byline), post-meta, and footer area on any Genesis theme.

WP Retina 2x
Make your website look beautiful and crisp on modern displays by creating and displaying retina images.

Page Builder by SiteOrigin
Build responsive page layouts using the widgets you know and love using this simple drag and drop editor.

SiteOrigin CSS
SiteOrigin CSS plugin.

Beaver Builder – WordPress Page Builder
The best drag and drop WordPress Page Builder.

Child Theme Configurator
When using the Customizer is not enough – Create a child theme from your installed.

AddQuicktag
This plugin makes it easy to add Quicktags to the html – and visual-editor.

Spacer
Adds a spacer button to the WYSIWYG visual editor.

Kirki
The ultimate toolkit for theme developers using the WordPress Customizer.

Responsive Menu
Highly customisable Responsive Menu plugin with 150+ options.

OptionTree
Theme Options UI Builder for WordPress. A simple way to create & save Theme Options.

Genesis Simple Hooks
This plugin creates a new Genesis settings page that allows you to insert code.

Cryout Serious Theme Settings
This plugin is designed to inter-operate with our Mantra, Parabola, Tempera, Nirvana themes to restore.

One-Click Child Theme
Adds a Theme option to any active theme allowing you to make a child theme.

Elementor Page Builder
The most advanced frontend drag & drop page builder.

Unyson
A simple and easy way to build a powerful website.

WP Responsive Menu
WP Responsive Menu turns your WordPress menu to a highly customizable sliding responsive menu.

SiteOrigin Widgets by CodeLights
Flexible high-end shortcodes and widgets. Responsive, modern, SEO-optimized and easy-to-use. Also can work without SiteOrigin.

Scroll Back To Top
This plugin will add a button that allows users to scroll smoothly to the top

Page Builder: Live Composer – drag and drop website builder (visual front end site editor)
Front-end page builder for WordPress with drag and drop editing. Build PRO responsive websites and…

Simple Custom CSS and JS
Easily add Custom CSS or JS to your website with an awesome editor.

WP PageNavi Style
Adds a more styling options to Wp-PageNavi WordPress plugin.

Genesis Title Toggle
Turn on/off page titles on a per page basis, and set sitewide defaults from Theme...

Any Mobile Theme Switcher
This Plugin detects mobile browser and display the theme as the setting done from admin....

Advanced Image Styles
Adjust an image's margins and border with ease in the Visual editor.

Child Themify
Create child themes at the click of a button.

Forget About Shortcode Buttons
A visual way to add CSS buttons in the post editor screen and to your...

Animate It!
Add cool CSS3 animations to your content.

Sticky Menu (or Anything!) on Scroll
Sticky Menu (Or Anything!) On Scroll will let you choose any element on your page...

What The File

What The File is the best tool to find out what template parts are used...

WPFront Scroll Top

WPFront Scroll Top plugin allows the visitor to easily scroll back to the top of...

Fourteen Colors

Not a big fan of green and black? Love the layout of Twenty Fourteen, but...

Nested Pages

Nested Pages provides a drag and drop interface for managing pages & posts in the...

Insert Html Snippet

Add HTML, CSS and javascript code to your pages and posts easily using shortcodes.

Simple Custom CSS

Add Custom CSS to your WordPress site without any hassles.

WP Add Custom CSS

Add custom css to the whole website and to specific posts and pages.

Simple CSS

Add CSS to your website through an admin editor, the Customizer or a metabox for...

MCE Table Buttons

Adds table editing controls to the visual content editor (TinyMCE).

Website Performance & Speed Plugins (10)

Autoptimize
Autoptimize speeds up your website and helps you save bandwidth by aggregating and minimizing JS.

P3 (Plugin Performance Profiler)
See which plugins are slowing down your site.

Compress JPEG & PNG images
Speed up your website. Optimize your JPEG and PNG images automatically with TinyPNG.

ShortPixel Image Optimizer
Speed up your website and boost your SEO by compressing old & new images and...

Cloudflare
All of Cloudflare's performance and security benefits in a simple one-click install.

Better WordPress Minify
Allows you to combine and minify your CSS and JS files to improve page load times.

Lazy Load
Lazy load images to improve page load times and server bandwidth.

Remove Query Strings From Static Resources
Remove query strings from static resources like CSS & JS files.

BJ Lazy Load
Lazy loading for images and iframes makes your site load faster and saves bandwidth. Uses...

WP Performance Score Booster
Speed-up page load times and improve website scores in services like PageSpeed, YSlow, Pingdom and

Widget & Sidebar Plugins (33)

Widget Importer & Exporter
Import and export your widgets.

Display Widgets
Simply hide widgets on specified pages. Adds checkboxes to each widget to either show or not.

Custom Sidebars – Dynamic Widget Area Manager
Flexible sidebars for custom widget configurations on every page, post and custom post type.

SiteOrigin Widgets Bundle
The SiteOrigin widget bundle gives you a collection of widgets that you can use and customize. All the widgets are built on our powerful framework, giving you advanced forms, unlimited colors and 1500+ icons.

Widget Logic
Widget Logic lets you control on which pages widgets appear using WP's conditional tags.

Image Widget
Image Widget is a simple plugin that uses the native WordPress media manager to add image widgets to your site.

Contact Widgets
Beautifully display social media and contact information on your website with these simple widgets.

Widget Logic
Widget Logic lets you control on which pages widgets appear using WP's conditional tags.

WooSidebars

WooSidebars adds functionality to display different widgets in a sidebar.

PHP Code Widget

Like the Text widget, but also allows working PHP code to be inserted.

Exec-PHP

The Exec-PHP plugin executes PHP code in posts, pages and text widgets.

Q2W3 Fixed Widget

Fixes positioning of the selected widgets, when the page is scrolled down.

Widget CSS Classes

Add custom classes and ids plus first, last, even, odd, and numbered classes to your site.

WP Tab Widget

WP Tab Widget is the AJAXified plugin which loads content by demand, and thus it.

Category Posts Widget

Adds a widget that shows the most recent posts from a single category.

Dynamic Widgets

Dynamic Widgets gives you full control on which pages a widget will display.

Simple Image Widget
A simple widget that makes it a breeze to add images to your sidebars.

amr shortcode any widget
Insert a widget or multiple widgets or a entire widget area (sidebar) into a page.

SMK Sidebar Generator
This plugin generates as many sidebars as you need.

Widgets on Pages
The easy way to Add Widgets or Sidebars to Posts and Pages using shortcodes or.

Enhanced Text Widget
An enhanced version of the text widget that supports Text, HTML, CSS, JavaScript, Flash, Shortcodes.

Widget Context
Show or hide widgets on specific posts, pages or sections of your site.

Simple Page Sidebars
Easily assign custom, widget-enabled sidebars to any page.

Widget Shortcode
Adds [widget] shortcode which enables you to output widgets anywhere you like.

Genesis Simple Sidebars
This plugin allows you to create multiple, dynamic widget areas, and assign those widget areas...

Widget Content Blocks
Edit widget content using the default WordPress visual editor and media uploading functionality.

Ultimate Posts Widget
The ultimate widget for displaying posts, custom post types or sticky posts with an array...

Awesome Weather Widget
Finally beautiful weather widgets for your beautiful site.

Content Blocks (Custom Post Widget)
This plugin enables you to edit and display Content Blocks in a sidebar widget or...

Content Aware Sidebars – Widget Area Control
Display custom sidebars on any post, page, category etc. Supports bbPress, BuddyPress, WooCommerce, Easy Digital...

PHP Text Widget
Executes PHP code on WordPress default Text Widget

Flexi Pages Widget
A highly configurable WordPress sidebar widget to list pages and sub-pages. User friendly widget control...

Flexible Posts Widget
An advanced posts display widget with many options. Display posts in your sidebars any way...

Video Sidebar Widgets
A collection of sidebar widgets for displaying Flash Videos from 14 video sharing networks.

YouTube & Video Plugins (5)

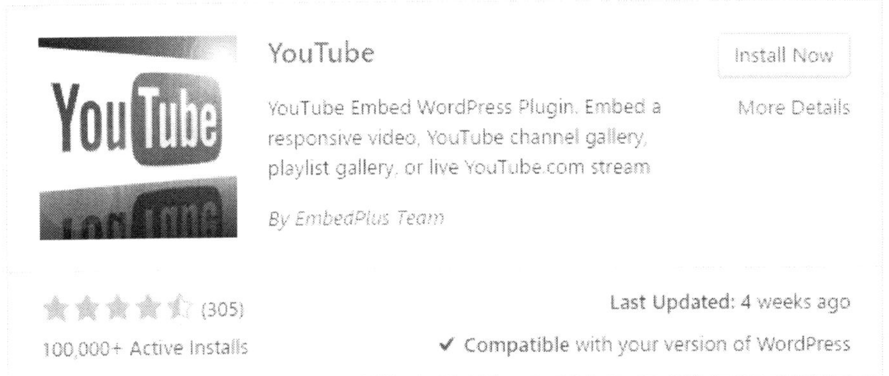

YouTube
YouTube Embed WordPress Plugin. Embed a responsive video, YouTube channel gallery, playlist gallery, or live.

YouTube Embed
An incredibly fast, simple, yet powerful, method of embedding YouTube videos into your WordPress site.

YouTube Widget Responsive
Share your channel with YouTube button subscribe.

WP Video Lightbox
Very easy to use WordPress lightbox plugin to display YouTube and Vimeo videos in an.

Gallery – Video Gallery and YouTube Gallery
Gallery Video plugin was created and specifically designed to show video links in unusual splendid…

BEST FREE IMAGE WEBSITES

I use a combination of images and videos to spruce up my sites. The videos are usually mine and from YouTube. To add a video, I copy the embed link then paste it on a page/post. Moreover, there are several video plugins that can help with embedding videos on your site.

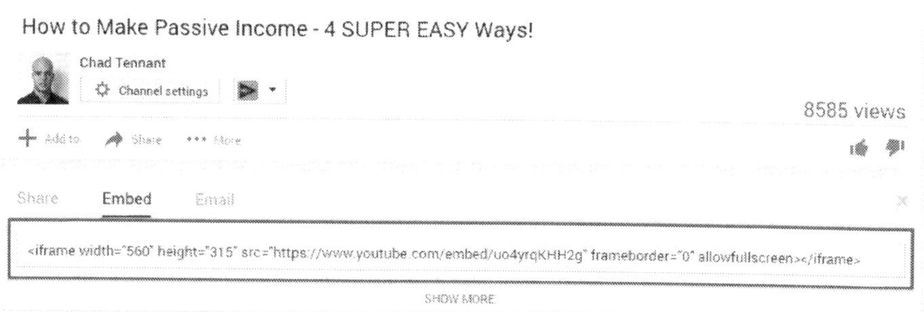

Since the early days of blogging, images have been in high demand. There was a time when excellent free images were hard to procure. However, in recent years, hundreds of free image sites have surfaced. Whenever using images that aren't yours, it's vital you that

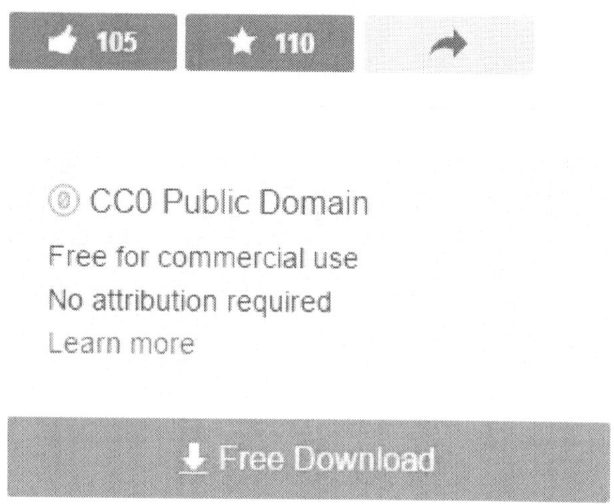

understand the rights and how you can use the images to avoid copyright infringement and fines.

Hubspot has a list of the "20 of the Best Websites to Download Royalty-Free Stock Images." Some of the sites I use made their list including Pixabay, Picjumbo, and Gratisography.

JOB SITES FOR WEB DEVELOPERS AND DESIGNERS

Some of you reading this book may be job hunting. There are several places you can look for web design/development opportunities as listed below. LinkedIn, and your network can also assist with your job search activities.

- 99Designs
- Behance
- Coroflot
- Dribbble Jobs
- Envato
- Fiverr
- Freelancer
- Guru
- Mashable
- Problogger
- Smashing Jobs
- We Work Remotely
- WordPress.net
- WPHired
- Upwork

I Invite You to Subscribe, Like, and Stay Connected for Additional Content

Chadtennant.com

http://www.chadtennant.com

YouTube

https://www.youtube.com/user/ChadTennantEVO?sub_confirmation=1

Facebook

https://www.facebook.com/chadtennantonline

LinkedIn

https://www.linkedin.com/in/chadeliottennant